T0145703

Testimonials

The Global Journey of an Asian is a fascinating story of hope, courage, and determination and learning the lessons of entrepreneurial life! Dr. Palan explores for us the lessons and gifts of his extraordinary entrepreneurial journey in his inspiring book The Global Journey of an Asian!

Marshall Goldsmith

2 million-selling author of the New York Times bestsellers, MOJO and What Got You Here Won't Get You There and the Thinkers 50 Award Winner (sponsored by Harvard Business Review) for Most-Influential Leadership Thinker in the World

Based on personal experiences, examples from business and politics, and written with passion and humility, this book is about defining your own success, knowing where you want to go but also being flexible and allowing life to take you in unexpected directions, connecting passion to purpose, truly understanding yourself and your strengths, being resilient, and the importance of continuing to learn. Dr. R. Palan takes everyone on his personal journey of learning, helping others to find their own practical individual applications.

Professor Boris Groysberg

*Richard P. Chapman Professor of Business Administration
Harvard Business School*

"Once you pick up this book, you live the UNLIVED potential of a human's heart and mind.. Once hard work is blended with a drive for GIVING, then all falls into place and one achieves. Palan's journey shared in these pages, sets any human's mind into a spree of daring plans for the future…HOPE is at the heart of the book but what is more important is the diligence behind this man's amazing life and the humility and simplicity that enabled him to REACH!"

Amal Ishaq Kooheji
Tamkeen, Manama, Bahrain

Palan was a source of inspiration for me to start my own Training business. As an executive in the corporate world,watching him in action,delivering workshops in a fun and impactful way was amazing. What also struck me was his ability to grow his business and people, combining passion and compassion! Combining one's passion with work,heart and fun became a distinct possibility for me after seeing Palan as an embodiment. I marvel at his ability to evolve and grow into different roles over the years allowing space for others. His personal example was a crucial factor that motivated me to take the leap into starting on my own.

Uday Khedkhar
Partner, LifeLong Learning Solutions India
Formerly with ICICI Bank, India

"Palan complements valuable lessons from his personal experiences with observations from an impressive range of academics, businessmen, and artists. His book is a must-read for anyone who hopes to become a successful entrepreneur, or who dares to grow in his personal and professional life."

Professor Ranjay Gulati
Jaime and Josefina Chua Tiampo Professor of Business Administration,
Harvard Business School

Entrepreneurship is a unique combination of human courage, imagination, adventure, self belief and sacrifice. It is always an inspiring story of human spirit succeeding in the face of multiple struggles. The outcome of such a journey is not just the economic success of a few individuals but also the creation of institutions that carries the imprint of the individuals' deep values and unparalleled efforts. It also creates an inspiring body of lessons for others who want to undertake a similar journey of human creativity.

Dr Palan's story captured in this book captures all the excitement of such a journey and more. It is also the story of a global citizen who broke through the barriers of culture, multiple regulatory environments and many other challenges. Dr Palan in writing the book has brought to the fore another facet of his entrepreneurship.

Santrupt Misra
Chief Executive Officer, Carbon Black,
Aditya Birla Group

"Palan's journey is not only a growth story based on bringing FUN into education but also a great guidebook on how to remain humble, keep your self-discipline and differentiate yourself from the crowd. Thank you Palan, I will be happy to apply several of your ideas in my own life."

Guido Kaelin
New Entrepreneur,
Former Vice President Marketing, Emmi of Switzerland

I have been fortunate to bear witness to Dr. Palan's journey of entrepreneurship and the enduring legacies resulting from his endeavor, as the SMR Group attests. As visionary and leader, Dr. Palan founded the Group on innovation and best practice principles, with his sight set firmly on achieving goals, despite the complex business and social climate in operation. His entrepreneurial spark has been fueled by his integrity, intellect, passion and creativity - a potent combination which has proved to be phenomenally successful.

Sally Rylatt
New Entrepreneur,
People and Organisational Development Professional
Formerly Project Manager, NAB Wealth, Australia

One of my favorite songs of all time is the late, great American singer Billie Holliday's, "God Bless the Child." It speaks to personal power, purposefulness and individuality - three amazing qualities that entrepreneurs must have. These are also qualities that Dr. R. Palan has benefitted from during his indefatigable entrepreneurial journey. Palan has lived a "no excuses" life and has turned that mindset and spirit into an incredible organisation that has touched thousands around the world!

Jim "Mr. Energy" Smith, Jr.
President & CEO (Jim Smith Jr. International)
Author (The No Excuse Guide to Success: No Matter What Your Boss
or Life Throws at You)

At my first meeting with Dato Palan, about six years ago, in my office in Singapore, I was taken in by his humility, for a man of his stature both as a professional and an entrepreneur. Why would he bother to visit me especially when I was just starting my journey as a L&D professional. This book truly reflects his philosophy of a true blue Asian professional embarking on his Global journey of entrepreneurship. There are many learning points in book that will unleash the passion of young and aspiring professionals who will be future entrepreneurs in a very connected world. A book written by an Asian for not only Asian readers but for the world to understand the complexities of the world today across generations and cultures. Great insights and an inspiring book."

Robert Yeo
Executive Director & CEO,
Singapore Training and Development Association

"This book is built around a unique personality. Palan exemplifies individuals with a unique vision. He is an extraordinary high performing individual , ever willing to share and one who has created rainbows for others. A truly important book that will help readers to feel, touch and achieve their dreams."

Dr. Ebrahim Al Dossary,
Prime Minister's Court, Kingdom of Bahrain
Past Chairman, International Federation for Training And
Development Organization (IFTDO)

The way Dr Palan speaks, writes and acts are consistently the same - passionate, highly intelligent and always value adding. His understanding of human psychology and how best people can significantly up their game, is the distinct reason why he continues to thrive in the tempestuous arena of entrepreneurship.

Tee Lin Say
Author of Faces of Fortune: The Twenty Tycoons To Bet On Over
the Next 10 Years.

In The Global Journey of an Asian, Palan shows how a journey can begin with a dream and you can grow by putting people first and profits second. He puts together the message of entrepreneurship with delightful personal anecdotes and lessons from great authors. A delightful book to read.

Datuk Seri Mohd Nadzmi Bin Mohd Salleh
Chairman, NADICORP Holdings Sdn Bhd
President Badminton Asia Confederation

"Palan crosses cultures effortlessly and this book will inspire others to imagine a world that celebrates diversity rather than try to accommodate it. Palan keeps himself abreast of latest practices in education and innovates to make learning a joy. "

Jugal Choudhary,
Director, MWH Global Inc

"For all those with the entrepreneurial fire, The Global Journey of an Asian, is a must read. Palan's Journey is a story about not being afraid to dream big and to passionately pursue those dreams without sacrificing your values. He provides excellent advice on how to successfully navigate the entrepreneurial waters."

Doug Murdock
President - Engineered Products Division.
Mueller Industries, Inc., USA

The Global Journey
of an Asian

The Global Journey of an Asian

The Entrepreneurial Journey of a Complete Outsider

R. Palan Ph.D.

Copyright © 2013 by R. Palaniappan

All rights reserved. No part of this book may be used or reproduced in any manner whatsoever without prior written consent of the author, except as provided by the United States of America copyright law.

Published by Advantage, Charleston, South Carolina.
Member of Advantage Media Group.

ADVANTAGE is a registered trademark and the Advantage colophon is a trademark of Advantage Media Group, Inc.

ISBN: 978-159932-487-6
LCCN: 2014935269

Most Advantage Media Group titles are available at special quantity discounts for bulk purchases for sales promotions, premiums, fundraising, and educational use. Special versions or book excerpts can also be created to fit specific needs.

For more information, please write: Special Markets, Advantage Media Group, P.O. Box 272, Charleston, SC 29402 or call 1.866.775.1696.

Dedicated to

My Family

my mum, Sethu Ramayee Achi

my wife, Kamu

my children, Maha, Subu and Shrieeya

who taught me that

no one is on a journey all alone.

And the best journey

is the one within yourself; one where you need to

let go of yesterday, be focused on the moment,

while looking forward to tomorrow.

Table of Contents

Foreword

His Excellency Honourable
Fidel V. Ramos
*President of the Republic of
Philippines, 1992 - 1998*

Entrepreneurship is tough; it is one of the hardest things to do. Being on your own and starting a business can be intimidating as any career plan. It involves tremendous personal commitment and determination. Yet, over 90% of businesses in Asia are in the small-and-medium category that includes informal ventures. Those who overcome the intense pressure have found success and some among them have gone on to reinvent the future. The challenge is always to sustain and grow the enterprise to the next higher level.

This is what drives entrepreneurial success. Because governments try to generate livelihood and employment for their people on a sustainable basis and adapt to meet challenges that arise, the future success of nations is bound to be rooted in entrepreneurship. Accordingly, it is Entrepreneurship that largely puts the power to control their own destiny back into the hands of ordinary people

The three virtues of **CARING, SHARING and DARING FOR OTHERS** needs to be naturally manifested within each of us who belong to ASEAN-10. All these attitudes require self-discipline, inspiration and courage. We must believe that work begins with ourselves.

Caring and Sharing are easy enough for the peoples of South East Asia to do because we are naturally friendly, hospitable, compassionate and even generous. But **Daring** is something else. It means **Daring** to struggle against overwhelming odds. Ultimately, **Daring** means to take united action in order to achieve the common good.

The best thing about writing a book is being able to provide a useful vision being informative, hopeful, and thought provoking; articulating best practices; cutting short the learning curve. Dr. R. Palan does all of these by deftly mixing personal anecdotes that are both practical and touching, together with positive actions that lead to success in a highly competitive world. He describes his life journey from a truly Asian perspective by defining some of the cultural factors that drive as well as inhibit success.

I have found Dr. R. Palan to be always passionate about **CARING, SHARING and DARING**. His devotion to writing despite his numerous corporate responsibilities and focus on recognizing people's meritorious achievements at the Asia Human Resource Development Awards is indeed admirable.

So let us read on!

March 13, 2006 – A proud moment - Hitting the gong at Bursa Malaysia Securities Berhad to take our company public. A memorable day, my heart skipped a beat seeing the shares race up from 33 cents to 61 cents. New and terrifying but very satisfying experience.

Prologue

. . .

March 13, 2006, is a day deeply etched in my memory. It was the day when I took my startup company public. As I stood in the corridors of capitalism, the Stock Exchange, and sounded the gong to signify the launch of the public trading of the company's shares, I was overwhelmed with emotions. The shares raced from its opening Initial Public Offering price to about double the value within a few minutes. While my mother, wife, children and well-wishers applauded the historic occasion in my life, I recalled that it had not been an easy journey. The journey of a professional trying to become an entrepreneur is a long and arduous one.

There are always contradictions in life. As a young person, I did not imagine myself being a capitalist, simply because as a young student I had discovered the basic tenets of Marxian ideology in the University walkways. The need for social justice was deeply ingrained within me. Ironically, today, here I am an entrepreneur, a capitalist. But, I've tried to be a capitalist with a heart. Just as oil and water don't mix, capitalist principles and social justice are not necessarily great allies. Yet when an entrepreneur demonstrates corporate social responsibility, it is a significant value contribution to the brand and the bottom line. My journey was driven by these principles.

I have been blessed with some good experiences and of course as in life with some difficult situations. Despite all the odds, I had made it on to here. This is the story of a global journey of an Asian professional who chose to become an entrepreneur.

Acknowledgements

. . .

The journey to write this book was a happy but long one. It took me a tremendous amount of time and effort to complete it. Given my multiple priorities in the last few years, it looked liked it will never end. I am now happy I finally completed it.

The strange thing about life is that we have to live it forwards but can only understand it backwards. That is the irony of life. My journey has had its share of difficulties, but I also paused several times to take in the joys of life as they happened. No one is perfect; we all strive for excellence. So have I.

As a perfect outsider in every culture that I lived in, I had to learn to engage with people and understand the joys of life. I learned very early in the journey that only I, not others, can make the journey for me. I had to bite the bullet and travel the distance. While others could support me, I had to be responsible for myself.

It is easy to get wrapped up in oneself and forget all those who made your journey possible. I have tried my very best at different points in my life to shore up my 'emotional bank account' with my colleagues, friends and family despite the many mistakes I made along the way. Each mistake was a learning point for me. There are many colleagues I'd like to thank and I will let that remain person to person. Here I'd like to single some who made this journey possible:

- Renu Joseph, my former colleague and book editor who partnered with me after 10 years and persuaded me to plod on and complete the book;

- Agnes Peter, my capable book designer;

- Chew Ann Nei, my executive assistant, who cleared time for me to complete the book;

- All the lovely people who work with me at SMR;

- Scott Friedman, a buddy who taught me the art of persuasion;

- Abdul Aziz, a friend who taught me the art of influencing people; and

- Last but not the least, my family for their love and support.

R.Palan

December 2013

*"It is never too late
to be what you
might have been."*

George Eliot

Introduction

On the Wings of Hope

. . .

Whether you like or dislike the policies of President Obama, you cannot but give him credit for his audacity of hope. When Barack Obama won the 2012 elections, in his victory speech, he reminded his supporters: "We did not win because of fate or luck; we won because of the hard work by all of you." His quest to become President in 2008 was an attempt to break the glass ceiling; he did it with hard work and a plan. There is a saying that success comes from 99% perspiration.

When he delivered the twenty-minute keynote titled The Audacity of Hope at the 2004 Democratic Convention, Obama was catapulted to national prominence. In his speech, he talked about hope, not blind optimism. He said, "I'm not talking about blind optimism here – the almost willful ignorance that thinks unemployment will go away if we just don't talk about it, or the health care crisis will solve itself if we just ignore it. No, I'm talking about something more substantial. It's the hope of slaves sitting around a fire singing freedom songs; the hope of immigrants setting out for distant shores; the hope of a young naval lieutenant bravely patrolling the Mekong Delta; the hope of a millworker's son who dares to defy the odds; the hope of a skinny kid with a funny name who believes that America has a place for him, too. Hope in the face of difficulty. Hope in the face of uncertainty. The audacity of hope."

It is this *audacity of hope* that helped me set out on my global journey too.

I could relate to the words of Obama. I didn't believe in blind optimism, nor did I wait for a stroke of luck to fall upon me. I certainly did not think that achieving my goals will be easy. My focus was on a journey with the hope that I could help people achieve their best through learning, and in the process, find a decent quality of life for my family. It was this passion that ignited my entrepreneurial spirit. It was this audacity of hope that pushed me to believe that I could succeed in adding value to the community and society that I lived in.

Some have the ability to succeed in what they want to do within a few years; others take much longer. Mine was a long journey but in the end, I did get where I wanted to be. I did it by wanting to be there, by design, by working with talented team members and with the support of family and well-wishers.

As I stood on the fringes of a new career as an entrepreneur, my thoughts raced back to an evening about thirty years ago and the ***defining moments in my life.***

You may agree or disagree with Obama's politics but no one can deny the audacity of his hope. He simply inspired me.

"We did not win because of fate or luck; we won because of the hard work by all of you."

President Barack Obama

Thirty Years Ago

...

It was late evening on a rainy Malaysian day. As it often happens with young graduates just out of University and unsure of what the future holds for them, I was in a deep thinking mode – or maybe another more reflective word would be 'a gloomy mode.' My classmate Nat, a liberal, was debating about the rationale of fairness in the world while I, a pragmatist as I defined myself then, sat slumped in the chair trying to figure out how to excel in what I liked to do.

Seated on the garden chairs adjacent to the then Bank Bumiputra building on Jalan Ampang, Kuala Lumpur, we watched the Klang river flow with fury. I needed to emerge out of the gloominess. So I forced a smile and said, "Nat, I have this funny feeling that one of these days, I will be a great success."

He burst out laughing with the words, "Good for you, but I do hope you know *what that success you are looking for is*." The day ended that way about 30 years ago.

A friend of mine, Uday Khedkar, always seeks to have *'crucial conversations'* for us to move forward with our lives. To me, this conversation with Nat was not only a crucial conversation but a defining moment in my life. I get sentimental when I recall this day after all these years.

When I look back at this journey, I wonder how I managed to achieve my goals the way I had defined them. Success has no single standard; wealth is not the only standard. It often involves defining what you want and going after that goal and achieving it. I could have collapsed many times over on this difficult journey, but I did not think so when I started out. The journey was commenced with a passion to achieve something in life and disprove the many sceptics who strongly held that I could never achieve my goals or that I would only be successful if I fit one of their paradigms.

This is the journey of an *ordinary outsider* – a chronicle of events of a professional trying to be an entrepreneur in the world of the soft sciences. It has been an awesome journey, exciting like a roller coaster ride. Not exactly the life of celebrities like Sir Richard Branson, David Beckham or Ian Botham, still challenging and adventurous in its own way.

This is one journey that proves the point that you can reach your dreams in your own way, simply being who you are and staying true to the purpose of your life. That is, if you figure it out at all what the purpose of your life is.

Many a time I have wondered if the journey would ever get started. Sir Michael Caine, nominated for the Oscars six times and winner of two, remarked that it was a long way from his origin – London's Elephant and Castle – to Hollywood. As he says, the shortest distance between two points is not always a straight line. My journey took me to about 30 countries. It certainly was no straight line, and sometimes the lines were so blurred that I thought there were none.

If I could sum it up, I would say it was all about *"Hope in the face of difficulty. Hope in the face of uncertainty. The audacity of hope."*

*"Hope in the
face of difficulty.
Hope in the
face of uncertainty.
The audacity of hope."*

President Barack Obama

Early Days

. . .

The irony is I never was quite sure where I belonged. The son of a Malaysian father and an Indian mother, I grew up in different countries. My father's ancestors migrated to what was then Malaya in the late 1890's. My father was born in India and came into Malaya via Burma (Myanmar). As it often happens with Indian families living abroad, marriage is a strategic alliance and takes place in India. My parents' marriage was no different.

I went to a Jesuit boarding school. Then, it was Pre-Medicals in a Lutheran college, followed by three years of undergraduate study in a college run by an Islamic trust. Finally I did my graduate studies in institutions that were dominated by freethinkers. I studied and worked in different countries, both Asian and Western. As my former colleague Jeremy Spoor would say with his dry British wit, "You were a mixed up kid." Probably this explains why I am a bundle of contradictions. Despite being a capitalist, I despise what capitalism sometimes does to accentuate poverty. Despite being entrenched deeply in the theories of psychology, I sometimes preach what I need to practise myself. Nevertheless, my *awareness of my own contradictions* has helped me grow into a better person. Or at least, that is what I believe.

Getting started meant *knowing myself and living in the moment.* It took me quite a while to figure out who I was before figuring out what I wanted to do in life. Some would say I had an eclectic upbringing. I didn't know then what it meant, but for sure I knew I had difficulty fitting in. 'Misfit' would have been the appropriate term.

My children make fun of my dislike for durians, the Malaysian choice fruit. Indian friends say I am not quite Indian as I do not follow sports such as cricket, the national passion in India. American friends ridicule me when they get to know I have never been to a football game. English friends sometimes sneer at my English pronunciation and Aussie colleagues chuckle at my poor seafaring abilities. So, 'misfit' is probably the correct word.

Nevertheless, being a misfit or finding myself being an outsider did not stop me from going on this global journey.

I did get started with great determination when I figured out what I wanted out of life. There were many colleagues who supported me in the pursuit of my goals in life, particularly in moments when I was about to give up. My journey was undertaken with lots of perspiration, some luck and lots of support from friends and family. It was simple, nothing out of the world, but I have enjoyed it immensely.

I had great joy watching the Indian movie *Three Idiots*. The movie about three friends chronicles their journey through life and it showcases the importance of living your life and the need to connect your purpose with your efforts. In the movie, Aamir Khan says "Connect your passion with your purpose and you'll be able to excel." The catch phrase in the movie *'All is Well'* aims to give credence to the belief that when you pursue your passion, all will be well.

Indeed, **all is well** and you are more likely to succeed when you connect your purpose with your efforts and follow through with sustained efforts.

Defining Moments in my Life

. . .

Defining Moments, Critical Choices and Pivotal People

While writing this book, I had several opportunities to reflect on my global journey and the decision I made to pursue the path of entrepreneurship. Dr Phil McGraw says that you can trace who you have become in life to ten defining moments, seven critical choices and five pivotal people. I would like to pause and recall the events, decisions and people that made me who I am.

Defining moments

In our life there are moments that impact our life, moments that open our eyes to new opportunities, where we learn something significant, a moment that pole vaults our career to help us realise our dreams and live the life that we truly want to live by design. These moments, both positive and negative, define and redefine you. Dr Phil McGraw says these defining moments penetrate your consciousness with such power that they change the very core of who and what you thought you were. A NEW you emerges as a result of experiencing that moment. In our lives, we experience these moments of truth that simply change the way we see things and offer us new insights. These new insights provide us with renewed self-confidence and courage to pursue things that we want in life rather than replay the daily routine, day in and day out. These defining moments are powerful change accelerators that enable us to let go of the past and move on to the new futures that we aspire for. Defining moments in life take place when we let go of conformity and fear. Defining moments enable us to take full authorship of our lives and lead us to peak experiences.

Critical Choices

I remember my psychology Professor M.T. Paul articulating psychologist Gordon Allport's definition of personality in his booming voice: Personality = Heredity x Environment x Time x Personal Choices. There are amazingly a very small number of personal choices that become critical choices and are game changers in our lives. Critical choices, irrespective of whether they are positive or negative, determine who and what you will become.

Pivotal people

Pivotal people are those who have left deep-rooted impressions on you and impacted your life. These are the people in your life who have influenced you strongly by changing your direction or path by something they said or what they represented. These are the people who inspired you to change, moulded you and helped you become who you are today. These are the people as Dr Phil McGraw says who can determine if you live consistently with your authentic self or instead live a façade controlled by a fictional self that has crowded out who you really are.

10 defining moments in my life

7 critical choices I made

5 pivotal people in my life

*"What lies behind us and
what lies before us
are tiny matters compared to
what lies within us"*

Ralph Waldo Emerson

10 *defining moments in my life*

1   Chance meetings lead to lifelong learning. Even short meetings may have a profound impact. One such meeting was with En Ahmad Pardas, the Managing Director of one of Malaysia's largest conglomerates, UEM. I gave him a copy of my book *The Magic of Making Training FUN!!* He received it politely and asked me, "Have you read the *Magic of Thinking BIG!?*" I hadn't, but when I read it, that single book had a profound influence on helping me think BIG! Thinking BIG is critical for entrepreneurs. His final statement as I walked out of his room still rings loudly in my ears: "If you want to be the person you want to be, you must walk, talk and behave like the person you want to be."

2 As I walked into the campus of Harvard Business School (HBS) in 2002, I felt a sense of awe. I thought to myself, a lover of Marxist philosophy had no business to be in this school that has developed some of the world's most successful capitalists. Yet, I learned so much about corporate social responsibility, social justice and value creation for the world at HBS. The experience I gained from HBS has pole vaulted my career, business and life. It is simply, as Dean Nitin Nohria says, transformational, an experience that opened my eyes to the world of possibilities and value creation.

3 It was a late rainy evening in Kuala Lumpur. There were just two of us in our office atop a shophouse. I asked my colleague Jeremy Spoor, much older, wiser and experienced than I, a question that reflected my nervousness. "Jeremy, do you think we should invest in talent management software?" His reply still resonates within me: "Palan, you must make the call, but you know that I am 64 years and I am incredibly excited." His excitement that evening led to my renewed self-confidence that defined us for the next decade.

4 My journey as an entrepreneur was triggered by a chance conversation with my uncle Maharaja at a sad

occasion: my father's funeral. The world had ended for me, but what my uncle said in his own way epitomised what Steve Jobs said: "Death is very likely the single best invention of Life. It is Life's change agent. It clears out the old to make way for the new. Right now the new is you." My uncle urged me to continue doing what I liked to do and not give up my dreams. His words were soothing at a painful moment when too many people were blaming my father for his entrepreneurial losses. That single conversation defined my outlook for the future.

5   I have always been conscious of the impact of cultures on the way people do business. One moment that jolted me was with Professor Christopher Bartlett leading the General Electric case study at the Harvard Business School. Not a great admirer of Jack Welch's staunch American management, I was a reluctant listener. Not for long though. The simple concept related by Jack Welch in a short video – 'Fix it, Sell it or Close it' when you have a floundering business – defined the way I looked at business and value creation. We had a few businesses that we were struggling to run profitably. After that one case discussion, we closed one business, sold another and fixed the rest with steadfast determination. I was spared of a lot of heartburn and mental fatigue.

6 Dr Nat is an ardent advocate of putting your thoughts on paper. He believes that there is a book within each one of us. I was reluctant to write as there were many who dissuaded me. But Dr Nat never gave up on me as a writer. He set up the systems for me to start writing and in due course I loved every bit of it. Writing my first book *The Magic of Making Training FUN!!* was an eye-opener for me. It created a NEW me, pole-vaulted my thought leadership and created opportunities that I could have never had before. Becoming an author gave me the authorship of my life in more ways than one.

7 The idea of taking our startup company public was a result of chance conversations with a few friends and well-wishers. Yet, the idea took fruition when Hj Ishak Hashim arrived unannounced at my office for a cup of tea. It was then I mentioned my thoughts about going public and the challenges. His immediate response was, "Let us not talk about it, let us do it now" and he placed the first call to the merchant banker. Within the next 24 months we were successful in achieving our goal. Going public defined our approach and outlook towards business and enabled us to run our business by design. That one conversation propelled our growth.

8   The concept of a blue ocean strategy, which emphasises doing business in uncontested markets rather than fighting for business in overly competitive markets, is popular today. A ninety-minute boat ride between Labuan and Bandar Seri Begawan taught me not only about blue ocean strategy, but also about the returns on investment for value creation. That visit to Brunei was a great learning experience as well as good business. One short boat trip spurred our long term success.

9   My first investor, Englishman Ed Jackson, would always underscore the need to grow through acquisitions and not just organically. It took me a long while to realise the importance of investing in value creating businesses, proving the adage that though life has to be lived forwards, it can only be understood backwards. When we started looking at acquisitions, we learned how much progress can be made through collaboration. Acquisitions taught me to look not just at the problem but also the opportunities that problems present. Often, when I talked with professional advisors, there was this inclination to look at problems and argue why we should NOT move forward. The strange thing about such an attitude is reflected in Helen Keller's statement, "I am nervous about people with vision not having a vision."

10 There is no greater defining moment than when children enter our lives. When you desire something and that eludes you, there is pain. Being childless for seven years was no different. The moment our first son was born, we were thrilled with joy and with our second son we were excited. And the joy was doubled when after an 11 year break our daughter arrived on the day I took our startup company public. Our children have taught us so much about life and love.

7 critical choices I made

1

Experimentation

I had met colleagues both from the United Kingdom and the United States of America who were experimenting with various business models to build a sustainable business. We had run a successful youth event called REACH and a few other successful conferences, but targeting an industry level conference seemed different and difficult. Yet, in the summer of 1985, we *chose to experiment* and run a high-volume low-cost conference called *Trainers Meet Trainers* with the unshaken confidence that we could succeed. In the pre-internet days, it was a great opportunity for networking. It was one critical decision that sustained the brand and the business. It was a significant game changer for us. There are numerous others who have copied the process and the name, but I am sure very few will ever be able to capture the passion.

2. Remaining Debt-Free

I haven't fully been able to take up motivational speakers' exhortations on the need to bounce back from failure. Yet, on the occasions when I experienced business failures and when recessions hit the economy, I realised the importance of another business school philosophy, also held dear by the Chettiar community, that *Cash is King*. The *decision to be debt-free* has largely helped us succeed even though at a much slower growth rate. And, of course we have been able to sleep well.

3. Networking

I am not an extrovert, but I remember the MBTI personality test training advice, "Do not let a personality trait or type stop you from doing what you want to." The Indus Valley network Malaysian chapter initiated by Tan Sri Gnanalingam is a movement designed to support entrepreneurs achieve their dreams. To me the decision to **attend one of the events** turned out to be lucky. The chance meeting with Emir Ruben Gnanalingam was a precursor to managing the intricacies of seeking credible investors. That single meeting opened up so many vistas of opportunities.

4 **Customer Care**

Customer care is good business and service recovery is important for the long-term growth of the business. One unsatisfactory training workshop with British Petroleum and the ***decision to do it all over again*** at no cost, despite short term losses was an invaluable decision. This single decision helped me engage the customer on so many fronts and the tremendous learning from this multinational customer laid the foundation for our ability to implement large scale projects in the years that followed.

5 **Following Your Heart**

I've read corporate success stories of entrepreneurship such as the time when Tan Sri Vincent Tan visited McDonald's Hamburger University and acquired the company's Malaysian franchise. In our case, training trainers was great business, yet we couldn't get a credible agency to accredit trainers internationally. I had a dream one day and decided to make ***a personal visit*** to the Institute of Training and Development, Beaconsfield, U.K. to persuade the Executive Director, at a time when we could not afford the cost. Finally in 1984, we were given the opportunity to launch the first Malaysian Certificate in Training & Development. It was a long and expensive trip, but a fruitful one.

6   Focus and Follow Through

You may disagree with the politics of Tan Sri Abdul Kadir Sheikh Fadzir, the former Tourism Minister of Malaysia, but you cannot disagree with his far-reaching ideas. He created the 'Malaysia, Truly Asia' campaign, thus putting Malaysia on the world tourism map. You have to admit that he has style. *I worked with him for a short while* but learned the value of his motto: *'Success comes with focus and follow through.'*

7   Navigating Politics

Dato Pardip Kumar, the handsome Chamber of Commerce enthusiast appointed me to head the Working Committee on HRD, ASEAN Chamber of Commerce. I learned about the world of global politics and the impact of Human Capital on a macroeconomic level. It was easy enough to learn that you can never run away from politics. My accepting the position reluctantly was the first step to learn how to manage global politics. It gave me a pedestal to shape policy and drive projects to accelerate business productivity and results. That single two year term helped me view politics differently.

5 *pivotal people in my life*

My family has had a tremendous influence on me. Sometimes I think that almost always we forget our families when we are asked who the most pivotal people in our lives are. So, even though there are numerous people who have had a great impact on me, I have restricted this list to people with whom I have had close interactions, such as family, work colleagues and teachers.

1 My mom

She knew that my dad was an enormous influence on me and my siblings. We were incredibly influenced by our dad. Yet, when he died at just 51 years of age, we were stunned. So was she. We had lost the only bread winner in the family. It was then that my siblings and

I realised the value of our mother. She just showed us love and care in her own way. She only spoke in Tamil to us, she was not overly patient, but she was the perfect role model of a strong woman.

Day in and day out, she taught us the value of discipline and persistence. She was there to pull us back every time we stepped over the line and taught us the value of living with honour. She taught us not to envy but to appreciate the success of other people.

Most of my focus and disciplined thinking is because of my mother. She taught me fiscal discipline and prudence. When I think about what has moulded me and how I got here on this global journey, it all comes back to the things my mom taught me. Most of who I am today as a person is because of my mom.

2 My grandfather

My maternal grandfather MPM Narayanan Chettiar and his brother-in-law, A Nagappa Chettiar, were renowned industrialists who single-handedly created the Indian leather industry as early as 1934. I have probably met my grandfather just a couple of times as we lived in different countries and he died when I was just a kid. Nevertheless, the impact he had on me was huge.

For starters he showed me that entrepreneurship is not just about making money but leaving a legacy and creating value for the country and society that you live in. He was absolutely clear about the purpose of being an entrepreneur. To him, success was not making it to the Forbes list even though he easily would have qualified to get in there. To him, it was about finding happiness in everything he did. He believed that wealth is not measured by the dollars in your bank account but by how rich your life is. He showed us the value of giving quietly and that giving is better than receiving. We learned the importance of compassion and understanding from him. Most of who I am today as an entrepreneur is because of him.

3 Sam Abishegam

Sam Abishegam was a doyen among Human Resources professionals. As a young graduate just out of the University and given the challenging economic and political times, I was desperate to get a job. Sam had retired, but he still gave me the opportunity to meet and work with him. He pointed out the numerous opportunities that lay right before me. When it looked to me like there was no future, he showed me the light at the end of the tunnel.

He was there to give me a pat and encourage me when I was low on self-esteem. He did all that he could to put me on a German scholarship with the Konrad Adenauer Stiftung. That one European trip changed the lens with which I viewed the world. What was important to him was what you could do, not what you couldn't. He was unequivocal that forgiveness is something never to be stingy with. I learned from this great man the art of consensus building and influencing skills. Most of who I am today as a manager is because of this great human resources professional.

Dr. Nat

Dr. Nat is a friend and a trusted work colleague who has this incredible skill of pushing you to do what you want to do. He showed me what it means to be a friend, how to agree to disagree and how to remain friends despite having differing points of view. He taught me the art of respecting people and making people feel included irrespective of race, religion, colour, gender or class. He is never one for generalisations; he stands out from many others with his relative objectivity. His deep incisive thinking and astute analysis means that you have to be prepared while engaging him in a conversation or debating with him.

He taught me how to go after what I wanted while still remembering who I am, whether it was writing my first book or going public. And more than anything, he pushed me towards the goals I had set for myself and made sure I knew what personal responsibility was all about. He helps me live my life authentically with his open feedforward and feedback and urges me every single day to live out my dreams. And that is exactly what I'm doing. Most of who I am today as a learner is because of this wonderful friend.

5 Father George Maliekal S.J.

I was packed off to a boarding school run by Jesuits while young. I resented this and I missed home while growing up, but the Jesuits showed me the value of self-discipline, learning and pursuing one's passion. Father George Maliekal was an amazing teacher who spotted my passion for arts and encouraged me in debate and drama. I learned from him that failure is the first step to success. The number of times I had failed on stage was enough to demotivate any young person. Most teachers would have decided that I was not good enough. Not Father George Maliekal. He would focus on closing the gaps I needed to succeed. He taught me that life is meant to be lived and fear is nothing to be afraid of. He drilled into me that giving up is never an option. He showed me how to love and care for people.

When I finally succeeded in debate and drama, I just could not help thinking what every kid would be able to achieve if they had teachers like Father George Maliekal. Most of who I am today as a professional is because of this wonderful teacher.

His Excellency Fidel V Ramos, Former President of the Republic of Philippines taught us that life is all about Caring, Sharing and Daring.

Her Excellency Datin Paduka Seri Rosmah Mansor; wife of the Honourable Prime Minister of Malaysia was the distinguished Guest of Honour at the Asia HRD Awards.

Time is always a scarce commodity when it comes to vacations. Finally got to the Taj Mahal with my mum and the family. Whoever said I don't practice work: life balance.

The Isaacs family in Ipoh, Malaysia. Great friends. A great source of emotional support when times were hard.

A special moment... the only time I ever attended a convocation. With my sons at the University of Leicester, U.K. Just wanted to stress the importance of lifelong learning to them.

Risk takers and visionaries - on my paternal side, my great grandfather (Ramanathan) and my grandfather (Palaniappan) lived in Myanmar and 'then' Malaya. They were risk-takers and visionaries. They travelled from India to Yangon, Myanmar and subsequently to Gemas, Malaysia. They gave me the 'entrepreneurial' genes.

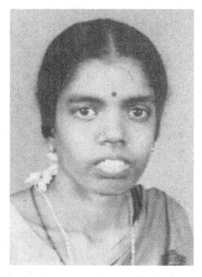

The nightingale of the family, my second sister. She died very young, just 29 years old, of post-partum hemorrhage, but not before she prepared me for the world. She taught me emotional intelligence and arithmetic problem-solving.

My maternal forefathers created the leather industry in India and globalised it. My grandmother's (Nachammai) brother A Nagappan with the Japanese leather industry leaders in the 1950's. They inspired my global mindset.

My grandmother and grandfather (Narayanan), second and third from right, were in quadrant four, the I's as Robert Kiyosaki defines it in his Cash Flow quadrant. Great investors, outstanding philanthropists and genuine believers in corporate social responsibility.

My dad (right) with a friend on one of his long walks in his plantation. He loved the solitude. Maybe my introverted personality came from him.

Documentation is critical. Simple and essential family practices.
a. The Myanmar business Rent Bill in 1940.
b. The Business Registration for the Gemas business in 1941.
c. The preferred bank, HSBC for grandpa even in 1942. We still bank with them.
d. Prudence starts with proper audit even in 1942

Memo

From

Registrar of Business Names, S.S.,
Supreme Court,
Singapore,

Date 10th July, 1941.
Mr. P.RM.P.
To Palaniappa Chettiar
5 Tampin Road,
GEMAS.

RENT BILL.

No. 163

Rangoon, _____ 194 .

Mr. _____ **Dr.**

To

P. RM. P. RAMANATHAN CHETTIAR.

118, Mogul Street, Rangoon

The Hongkong and Shanghai Banking Corporation

(INCORPORATED IN THE COLONY OF HONGKONG). THE LIABILITY OF MEMBERS IS LIMITED TO THE
EXTENT AND IN MANNER PRESCRIBED BY ORDINANCE NO. 6 OF 1929 OF THE COLONY

MALACCA 31 DEC 1942 19 ____

P.R.M.P. Palaniappa Chettiar
5. Tampin Road
Gemas. N.S.

231

July 16, 2602 **194** 2

P.R.M.P (Rama Rawanna Mana Pana) Firm,

No.5, Tampin Road, Gemas. **Dr.**

To

KESAVAN & Co.,

ACCOUNTANTS & AUDITORS.

No.29, Hicks Road, Kuala Lumpur

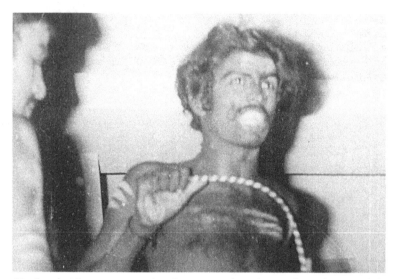

Tried to break into acting when I was a student during the early part of the journey. As the picture indicates, guess I was a failed actor. Learned to move on.

In 1989, at the University of Chicago with my brother, a Chicago resident. Different journeys but still close.

At the 1988 American Society of Training & Development when BP won an award for their people development excellence. Working on assignments with BP pushed me to think differently.

In 1992, my first successful road show to several cities in China and Hong Kong. It was the dream of every person to break into the China market then.

CHAPTER 1

The Dream

. . .

What is that success you are looking for? Do you dream about it? Can you visualise it?

Most of the time self-help authors and motivators talk about connecting to one's life purpose. Jim Collins, in his book *Good to Great* , talks about the Hedgehog Concept. The Hedgehog concept is not a goal to be the best, not a goal to excel in something, in the sense of doing it better than everyone else, but it is largely about **understanding what you can be best at.** When Dr. Nat said he hoped I knew what my success was going to be, to me it was largely trying to understand what I could be best at.

My goal has been to figure out areas that I could excel in. As I was very passionate about helping people learn, I pursued a career in helping adults learn and contributing to that body of knowledge. I pursued my passion because I never saw it as work, but as a part of my life. The luxuries of life such as a better house or car came along as by-products of my core goal of helping adults learn. My dream was to excel in helping adults enjoy and benefit from the learning. I learnt at least six simple lessons along the way.

The first lesson was to grow by *learning from mistakes* or experiences. As the great management author Peter Drucker has said: "Mistakes occur but do not let them recur." I've made many mistakes but I always remember the saying – no one learns without making mistakes. I had to gain the confidence to make mistakes, in safe and supportive environments, to achieve my dream. I had some great teachers and coaches who enabled me to learn from mistakes and use the experiences to grow into a more mature professional.

The second lesson was learning to break down *complexity into simplicity*. Whenever I looked at a concept, I always believed it could be made much simpler. Making something simple doesn't mean it is simplistic – or simpler than the way things actually are. Steve Jobs believed in the concept of simplicity. The simplicity that Apple talked about was a result of deep complex thinking. Somebody did some complex thinking so that a simple, easy to use gadget could be made. Dr. Nat always says, "Just because something looks simple and friendly doesn't mean that it is simplistic. A lot of thought has gone into it to make it look simple." That was my passion. How can I make learning easier for people? Can I teach people in a better way? Can I make learning FUN?

The third lesson was that **connecting passion to purpose** is critical. Success happens when you figure what you can be good at. The benchmark is what we are capable of, not being someone else. Unfortunately, people clamour to be appreciated for the one thing they can't do well, rather than be complimented for the 99 things they are good at.

The fourth lesson was the need to **evolve into new roles** as we grow. I loved helping people learn and grow to enable them to become highly productive at the workplace. I carried on with the profession. But of course, as I grew, I realised the need to evolve. I desired to be an entrepreneur too because I came from an entrepreneurial family. That was another one of my dreams.

The fifth lesson was about **sharing experiences to grow** into a more productive person. Many times after I wrote the book *Creating Your Own Rainbow*, a book that described some of my life experiences, people have asked me, "Well, we understand how you did it. But could you give us a framework for success?" Honestly, most of that framework is primarily very tacit. I couldn't really put it in words for a long time. I hope in describing my global journey as a person who has been educated in different parts of the world, but is largely Asian in his values and outlook, I will be able to make some of those ideas in my head a little bit more explicit. But honestly, I don't think I have a framework. I have no magic formula. My journey worked out well for me. What I can share are my experiences and some of the universal principles that have worked around the world, which anyone can put to good use.

The sixth lesson was that reaching your goals takes a *series of steps*. I remember an analogy a famous author once talked about. A company or an individual toils for years together and one fine day there is success and people rave about how they have arrived. The writer compared the situation to that of an egg hatching. One of the biggest moments to the outside world is when an egg cracks and the chick comes out. But when you look at it from the perspective of the chicken, the cracking is just a small step in a long journey. Unfortunately, that is the only step the outside world is aware of. I think that reaching your destination is a series of small steps. For example, taking my company public did not happen at one go. That was an outcome of several steps.

Integrating these six lessons into my life and understanding that *success is not one-dimensional* was important for me in my global journey. There are several ways to look at success. I think of success as setting out to do something and achieving it. It involves making a contribution to someone else's life, adding value, and in the process, achieving for oneself a decent quality of life. It isn't about becoming the next billionaire in town, which I certainly am not, nor is it about finding happiness in being poor. It is about making sure that one does make a contribution to the profession, organisation, community and nation. Success is thus creating value not just for yourself, but also for others. In the process of creating value for someone else, I can create value for my family and myself by having a certain quality of life. To me that is success.

Thus while I focused on honing my personal skills, I also started exploring how I could develop an organisation. That is how I started an organisation 30 years ago in something that I thought we could add value without putting too much pressure on ourselves. It was my personal belief that I would enjoy the focus on workplace training, as at that point in time I believed that starting a university or a college was an unaffordable option. So we went on to build and develop an organisation in workplace training.

Did I plan every step of the way or did paths just open up before me as I went along? I just don't know but I would say the ultimate goal was always quite clear. I just had to go through the various steps. I didn't reach my goals overnight. It was as Lao-Tzu says: "Every step is a small step in a long journey."

I was not aware when we started that we would move into offices in the Central Business District or go public, but on reflection, I do think we had some clear goals to guide us. Sometimes people used to laugh when we shared our goals or dreams with them. Nobody can actually tell you not to dream. When I started off, I had this poster in my room:

"When you have a dream,
Don't let anything dim it,
Keep hoping, keep trying,
The sky is the limit."

A lot of my colleagues seem to take this very casually today. Some of those who moved into my office recently, promptly moved this poster to the most inconspicuous place in the office. I had to work hard to get the poster back into an area where it could be seen prominently.

You just have to keep trying, keep going and the sky is the limit. I like Jim Collins' concept of ***Big Hairy Audacious Goals (BHAGs)*** which are big, bold, powerful long term goals. In my case, I always had some BHAGs. I always wanted to run a larger company that contributed to nation building. I wanted to operate out of our own building. I always wanted to go global, speak in many countries, launch new products, and write new books. It was always a question of prioritising and just doing what we needed to do.

"When you have a dream,
Don't let anything dim it,
Keep hoping, keep trying,
The sky is the limit."

In a global journey, it is foolhardy to ignore your personal growth. This is one of the things I learned from the book *Good to Great* where Jim Collins says that good is the enemy of great. He says that success or greatness comes to companies because of what they do to themselves, rather than what the world does to them. Everywhere around the world, people talk about economic recessions, the slowing global economy, the challenges in Greece and Spain. To me, it is important to know that we need to excel in what we do to be great. This will cushion the impact of negative external events.

Even in challenging economic conditions there are people who do well. It happens because they know exactly what they want and are passionate about it. They are not in the rat race, but outside of it, competing with themselves to excel. So, personal growth and the growth of those around them are extremely important for entrepreneurs embarking upon a global journey.

CHAPTER 2

Getting Started

. . .

Like most young people venturing into the world of entrepreneurship, I had a lot of dreams. However as I was just getting started, every day was a sort of reality check. You dream at night and when the day starts, you realise that it is not exactly unfolding the way you wanted it to.

The hope that everything will be okay is almost always false for the one who is just getting started on an entrepreneurial journey as some surprises are always in store. You think you are going to get this big contract with a certain company, only to find your initial optimism waning. You go into their corporate office with tremendous energy, which soon dissipates when you find that there are so many other people out there. The fear that you cannot succeed when the big boys or branded consulting companies are there overwhelms you. You conclude that you are not going to win the contract. As Don Kirkpartick, the legendary training evaluation guru says, "You are already two goals down before the game has begun."

I soon realised that competition was a way of life and being an entrepreneur simply meant that I had to deal with it. More harmful than the threat that competition actually posed was what I allowed it to do to my mind. The problem lay with how I regarded competition than what it actually was. It quickly became clear that self-esteem and self-worth are essential ingredients for an entrepreneurial journey. I came to recognise that if I wanted to compete with some of the leaders in the industry, *the simple premise was that I needed to excel in what I did, even if I was not the world's best.* If I wanted to win the game in the markets I served, I had to have a strategy, the competence and a drive to excel.

I kept it simple when I started out in the field of corporate training. I chose to remain focused on running a few training programmes a year aimed at the junior management level. I brought in experts from within and outside Malaysia.

As I got deeply entrenched into running the business, I swiftly recognised that I didn't have the tools essential to succeed in business. I had an abundance of passion and I was aware of my life purpose, but I didn't have a business, financial or marketing plan. Without a focused plan, I found myself immersed in ad hoc activity that stressed me out. I also found that despite having studied about human behaviour, I lacked the business sense to decide who I could do business with and who I should avoid. Very soon, I found out that I had lots of bills to pay without recurring revenue. I was beginning to experience what every entrepreneur dreads: a cash flow squeeze. The need for entrepreneurial common sense as well as some critical business tools made me seek help from my well-wishers and mentors. I realised that without these, passion and purpose will be of no use on my entrepreneurial journey.

My mentors set me some simple goals. First, I had to establish my strengths and weaknesses in terms of business skills and tools. Then I had to go out and acquire the necessary skills, either formally or informally. They emphasised the need for informal learning time and again. My attempts helped me learn six important lessons in my early days on this journey.

First, I learned *to work with people who are different from me.* Working with people different from us is an important skill. We do not find very many like ourselves on a global journey. Being comfortable with diversity helped me deal with different cultures even within a small region. My limited backpacking experience, though unusual in Asia, helped me greatly when working with people from different cultures.

Second, I learned *the value of being humble in the quest for learning.* Humility is a great teacher. I have observed the sense of humility in some of the greatest entrepreneurs and teachers. As a Zen Master has remarked, you learn nothing when you are full. You have to be open to learning. As a famous quote goes, "Minds are like parachutes, they only function when they are open." Unless a person is humble, they are unlikely to be open to new insights and experiences.

My journey started when I parked myself as an assistant to great teachers and started learning from them. Most of them were very willing to help me learn and grow. This safe environment helped me gain confidence. Not everyone is blessed with developmental opportunities provided by organisations or governments. We have to engage in our own learning. In my journey, I found the opportunities to observe and learn from some of the greatest teachers very rewarding. One of them was the late Professor Dean F Berry of Insead and another was a Jesuit priest, Father Leonard Paul who was my teacher.

While financial and marketing skills can be learned formally through courses, these great leaders taught me some important life skills. Such informal learning is invaluable. For instance, they demonstrated the importance of being assertive without being aggressive. To a person like me who is very uncomfortable with any assertiveness, this learning through observation was priceless.

"Minds are like parachutes, they only function when they are open."

Learning from observation is a powerful vehicle for growth. While I learned about reconciling a bank statement in a training session, observing an accounts clerk reconciling a bank statement and learning from her helped me see how it is done in the real world. My late father had time and again emphasised that you can learn anytime from anyone and everyone if only you choose to. The pursuit of learning requires openness, humility and observation.

My professors in college said that getting started and sustaining yourself on a global entrepreneurial journey comes from the ability to observe. Great entrepreneurs observed the changes in the world, in their organisation and in the national, regional and international economy.

Third, I learned the value of *seeking feedback for personal growth.* This is especially tough when you take the criticism directed at your shortcomings personally. Just like most other people, it was indeed very tough for me to take sharp criticism, but my mentors were excellent in the way they coached me to both give and receive feedback. To an entrepreneur, the ability to receive feedback in a positive way is important for personal and business growth.

As I got started and gained some confidence, I was ready to take some bold steps on my own. I continued to make cold calls and sought to sell our training programmes to larger customers.

At that time, a leading petroleum multinational offered me the opportunity to conduct a training programme for their dealers. As I felt rather inadequate to run the workshop, I sought the help of an experienced colleague to lead the workshop. To my dismay, the workshop was an utter failure. The organisation felt that their investment in the training initiative had been wasted. Apparently, the experienced colleague and friend of mine had not made an effort to first understand the company's needs and therefore could not add value to them.

As a student, I had learned the value of customer service excellence and customer retention for business success. Professor Kirkpatrick's four level evaluation model was a useful guide:

- Were you happy with the programme?
- Did you learn something of use?
- Can you implement what you learned?
- Can the learning improve the results?

I made a follow-up service call to the customer, a young Australian manager. I had always rightly or wrongly viewed Australians as very assertive, and I used to be particularly wary of young Australians as my few interactions left me with the impression that they were straight and blunt in stating facts.

The young Australian manager did not mince his words. He answered 'NO' to every one of Don Kirkpatrick's four questions and explained in a very factual manner why the programme was one of the worst he had ever attended in his entire career. To him and his 25 colleagues, it was an absolute waste of time.

That was valuable feedback, but I found it very difficult to take. The good thing was that my learning helped me not to be offended with the frank feedback. I had two options before me. One was to tell the customer that they can have all of their money back. Unfortunately, I was running a small business and I had already used up the money. My other option was to offer something else to the customer. After much thought and hesitation, I offered the customer a choice. I said, "Well, if you give me the opportunity, I will personally run the programme for you." I still don't know why I said that because in the first instance, I hadn't had the confidence to run it. However, the feedback from the customer indicated the problem was the unwillingness of the other trainer to listen to the customer's needs. I thought I could handle that with some preparation.

The young manager was surprised and asked: "Are you willing to invest another two days at no further cost?" Unhesitatingly, I said, "Yes, absolutely." The customer agreed for us to work together. I spent a week trying to find out the needs of their dealers and completely customised the training programme. I ran that programme to the satisfaction of the customer and that gave me an introduction to his counterparts in other countries.

That single customer service call and the willingness to take the feedback got me started on my global journey. If that call had never been made, I wouldn't have got the feedback that made me offer to redo the programme. I did not think of it as a cost, but as an investment. This investment led to a seven-year relationship, a very profitable and professionally satisfying one. I never forgot the value of feedback and the fact that the best advertisement is word of mouth and referrals from existing customers. I personally took much away from that experience.

It gave me an exposure into the workings of a large multinational. It also helped me communicate with and relate to people who were culturally different from me. Finally, as it was a successful programme, it gave a tremendous boost to my self-confidence. It was a win-win situation.

The customer had lots of information on customer service, but they preferred to leave dealer training to someone with the specific expertise and process skills to do that. My work with the customer continued over the next seven years. In marriage they say there is a seven-year itch. Probably it works in the case of business relationships as well. The customer's business was evolving and so was my training business. My growth was accelerating in terms of business volume and so I could not have that direct relationship with the customer. The relationship tapered off gradually, but not before I had the opportunity to work with the organisation in other countries such as Singapore and Hong Kong. It gave me a wonderful glimpse into what a global journey could look like.

Fourth, *the need for entrepreneurs to take risks* dawned upon me. In business, success is about changing with changing times and doing new things. However, there are risks associated with doing new things. My mentors taught me the value of managing risks as they are part of business. My global journey took me to new territories. To me, working with cultures and countries different from mine was a valuable experience. Instead of working within just one culture, going global meant I could work with different cultures and experience new ways of doing business.

In one situation, I had a predominantly Chinese audience. It was a customer service programme for the dealers of the petroleum company that I mentioned earlier. The participants were not employees, but businessmen. The dealer network, which was dominated by the larger oil companies, was going through a significant change at that time. My customer was a small player and there were other local players coming into the business. While the training focused on customer service, the trainees were business-focused dealers concentrating on revenues. I thus had to deliver a training programme with the objective of improving customer service, which at the same time also met the objectives of an audience focused on revenue.

It was a time when oil companies could not promote petrol using pricing strategies as it was a controlled item with a fixed price. Retail marketing of petrol was not that easy. What you could differentiate was in making customer service a pleasant experience. It wasn't difficult to copy these practices from someone else. So if one dealer cleaned windscreens or completed a simple and basic check under the hood, another dealer could just as easily do the same. Still, when you trained staff for delivering good customer service consistently, there was a definite competitive advantage.

Another challenge was in service delivery. In Malaysia, it was easier because young people were staffing petrol stations. In some countries within Asia for example Singapore, at that time, older people were employed in these jobs because the younger generation did not find working in a service station an interesting career option. Singapore was such a fast-paced society. As soon as people got in to the station, they wanted to get out, but they would be served by an older person whose reflexes weren't very quick.

Culturally too there were difficulties. In some cultures, saying good morning isn't a way of life but the customers, especially those from the West or exposed to the Western culture, expected to be greeted with a smile.

So while appreciating some of the cultural nuances,

it was important to get across this message to the business-focused audience: "It doesn't matter what you think is your cultural norm, but if you want to be in business, you just need to give what the customer wants."

Together with the customer, we worked on strategies to get the message across to the audience. I wasn't creating anything new at all. The customer had a huge amount of resources internally. I just had to take these resources and use some process skills to get the message across in an easy to understand manner.

It turned out that the dealers were quite excited to learn when they found that their needs were being addressed and they knew they could use what they had learned in the programme to make an impact to their bottom-line.

Fifth, *I learned the need to have a Blue Ocean Strategy*. The concept of *Blue Ocean Strategy* gained prominence with a path breaking book by Professors W. Kim Chan and Renée Mauborgne. Yet, I guess, there were entrepreneurs and organisations practicing the principles of Blue Ocean Strategy long before the book was published. In this game-changing book, the authors argued that companies engaging in head to head competition for sustained profitable growth are unlikely to succeed. Such a move, they argued is unlikely to gain them competitive advantage, differentiation or market share. On the other hand, they claimed, such approaches only lead to bloody 'red oceans' of competitors fighting over a dwindling profit pool. This book challenged the notion of strategic success as defined traditionally. They stressed the need to focus on creating 'blue oceans' of uncontested market space leading to unfettered growth. Such an approach, they argued, is the systematic way forward to create a sustainable profitable growth. The focus moves away from competition to value creation. They highlighted six principles. The six principles show how to reconstruct market boundaries, focus on the big picture, reach beyond existing demand, get the strategic sequence right, overcome organizational hurdles and build execution into strategy. Blue Ocean Strategy is all about charting a bold path to winning the future.

As I found the local economy and market getting difficult, I needed to figure out what I had to do differently. There were suggestions that I should venture out into developed markets such as Singapore, Hong Kong or even the United Kingdom. These markets were very competitive and in my view, the training markets in these locations were saturated. I chose to follow a different path, explore the market in Brunei, the tiny oil rich kingdom nearby.

Many years ago, when I had finished my Masters, I had an opportunity to visit Brunei. Most of what I knew about Brunei at that time was that its Sultan was the richest man on earth. At that point the Brunei government wanted to hire good quality people. So sometime in 1980-81, my classmate Dicky Maniam and I landed up to interview for a position in the counselling department at the Brunei capital's General Hospital. Dicky was a very passionate psychotherapist and counsellor. He came very prepared for the interview, unlike me. My passion was in workplace education. To cut a long story short, it wasn't very difficult to make a choice between the two of us. He got the job. But during my visit, I noticed that Brunei was a land of opportunities. That observation stuck firmly in my mind. Later in 1984, the country gained independence from the British.

With the Malaysian economy getting difficult and everyone cutting prices, it soon became apparent that it was one of those situations when everybody became either a consultant or a trainer because of the low entry barrier. So I had to go out and find new opportunities or recreate myself. It was at this point that I found the efforts of the Government timely: export of services was being promoted vigorously. I recalled my observation about Brunei.

To explore another country and to venture into a new market meant taking risks, establishing relationships, reviewing opportunities and executing plans flawlessly. These were principles that I preached, along with the need for everyone to change with changing times. It was time for me to reinvent myself. I recall the quote attributed to many people, including Abraham Lincoln, Alan Kay and Peter Drucker: "The best way to predict the future is to create it." As Kim and Mauborgne wrote in the *Blue Ocean Strategy*, the key to winning the future is to avoid competing in the red ocean because it is all about killing one another and move on to the blue ocean. Strangely enough, my next stop had to do with crossing an ocean, visiting Brunei with the purpose of exploring the Brunei training market.

After the experience with the petroleum multinational, I started working in Labuan, with a large integrated manufacturing company, I happenned to visit the ferry terminal where I saw boats heading for Brunei. I knew that Brunei worked on Saturdays but not on Fridays and Sundays. My customer worked Monday to Friday. I had Saturdays off. I decided that I had to get to Brunei. This was a great opportunity – I was so close to Brunei. When I had gone there almost eight years earlier, I had flown through Singapore which at that time was the only way to get there. Brunei was just a short ferry ride from Labuan. So I headed for the ferry terminal, which looked like a boat jetty. I enquired where I could find a ferry to Brunei and was pointed in the direction of what looked like a fishing boat with an outboard motor. I was told that it was just a 30 minute ride – nothing to get worried about.

I asked, "Where do I get the ticket?" "Just jump in and pay the money," came the quick reply. It was about 20 ringgit or so. I thought it was incredibly cheap. I got in, paid and asked for the ticket, the boatman said not to worry as there was no such thing. I was perplexed when he asked for another 10 ringgit as I had already paid for the ticket. This time, I was told, the money was for the diesel. The boat carried about 20 people. It had no shade to shield the passengers from rain or shine. We soon hit the high seas and every time the boat hit the waves, it looked like we were about to go under. Recollecting that experience now, I get very worried. It was such a compromise on safety that I wouldn't dare to attempt that ride today. However, then I was young, keen to look for opportunities wherever I could find them and that ride didn't seem all that scary. Finally, to my great relief, we landed in Brunei safely.

I had done some research using the few resources available in the pre-internet days. And I knew that there were only three major employers. I went to meet my first Bruneian prospect. To my surprise, I was asked to make a presentation almost immediately. I had come prepared for the event. I pulled out my overhead slides and presented an overview of my capabilities. I was happy that they liked what they saw. With the introductions done and the business sealed, conversation became more social. They were curious as to how I had flown into Brunei. I said I had not and related my boat ride from Labuan. Laughing, they told me they called these boats 'death boats' because of the number of accidents they got into. On hindsight, I think I should have found a better way to get there, but anyway I had survived the journey. I had met the right prospect and secured the business. I worked with the Bruneian customer for the next 10 years surviving the seven-year rule that afflicts business relationships.

I had not only got into a new and uncontested market space but had also found new ways to build a business. Robert Kiyosaki's 'Cash Flow Quadrant' in his book *Rich Dad Poor Dad* is a very powerful tool. He details the four concepts exceedingly well:

- **E** – employees who value security as they prefer a safe and secure job
- **S** – self-employed business owners who prefer to go solo and do everything themselves
- **B** – business entrepreneurs who get smart people to run the business for them and value good systems and networks
- **I** – Investors who have money working for them

I realised that I had moved from the E and S quadrants to the B. I had to run to my colleagues in the business to help me deliver this huge project. I could have never done it solo. The concepts of scalability and non-linear income were beginning to make enormous sense to me. When my colleagues and I had trained several thousands in Brunei, I realised that I had moved on from being a trainer to an entrepreneur in

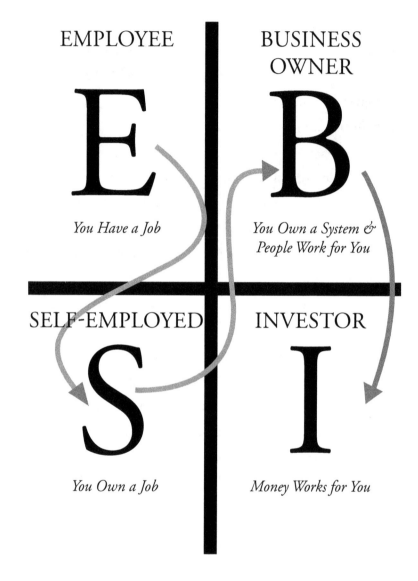

EMPLOYEE

BUSINESS
OWNER

E | B

You Have a Job

You Own a System &
People Work for You

SELF-EMPLOYED

INVESTOR

S | I

You Own a Job

Money Works for You

Robert Kiyosaki's *'Cashflow Quadrant'* in his book *Rich Dad Poor Dad*

the training business. The training focused on a whole range of management skills to help people become more productive. After dealer training and customer service, now I was working with senior management trying to bring about change and a new organisational culture focused on high performance and productivity.

Brunei was a new market, which was uncontested and at that time completely open. It was a great experience for me. Again, it was *the audacity of hope* that took me to Brunei. It was not just luck or my being there at the right time and the right place. It was a thought out process. On hindsight, I wish I had observed more inflection points (changes that an entrepreneur can benefit from) or moved faster. Nevertheless, as Soren Kierkegaard pointed out, "Life must be lived forward, but can only be understood backwards." At that time, I was happy that I had at least achieved my goal of getting into a new market.

Brunei was my fourth country after Singapore, Malaysia and Hong Kong. It certainly was very different. It wasn't an MNC atmosphere or culture. It didn't have the fast pace of Singapore. Brunei sported a very laid back culture infused with the values of respect, honesty and humility. As they had just gained independence, there was a tremendous drive to develop local Bruneians at a young age. It gave me a great opportunity as the appetite for learning among the Bruneians was huge. I could thus play a far more significant role in helping them learn.

However, I also had to learn to let go of cultural stereotypes which defined productivity as working nine-to-five or being 110% committed to work. In Brunei, family takes precedence over work. When I was working there, at 12 o'clock the whole of Brunei came to a stop because everybody had to go and pick up their children from school. No matter how important the point you were making was, at 12 noon people would say, "Thank you very much, my kids are far more important." At 4 pm, we stopped again. So I found that I needed to adjust to the Bruneian clock, trying to understand what their needs were. Between 8.00 and 12.00 in the morning and 2.00 and 4.00 in the afternoon, I had such committed learners. But nothing could invade family time. That was my learning in Brunei. As an entrepreneur and a training professional, I learned so much from my Bruneian participants.

Over the next few years, the Brunei market started attracting competitors. As they came along, I found that I had to vacate some of the market space because I wanted to move up the value chain. In the late 90's, my long term relationship with Brunei slowly tapered off. But those ten years of learning about a new culture and a new way of learning were great. Brunei was an uncontested market, but it was never going to be that way all the time. New players and new competitors were bound to appear. Change happens to every person in every business in

"Life must be lived forward, but can only be understood backwards."

Soren Kierkegaard

every market. The sooner we understand it, the better it is for the sustainable profitable growth of the business.

Finally, I learned the need for *executional excellence.* Around this time, I had the opportunity to work with a reasonably large Malaysian financial services company. It was a very different experience compared to the oil company or the Bruneian experience. The company was very laid back, while the industry was very competitive. The sales force had to be trained in building strong bonds with customers because people bought intangible products based on trust and relationships. For some years I had been doing some work with them in training. At this particular point, I had the opportunity to work on a strategic plan for the company together with a leading strategy consultant.

I was now beginning to move up the value chain as I was moving away from training to consulting work on business issues. I was able to get a glimpse into the inner workings of the company. That was when I realised that however good a plan you draw up and deliver as a consultant, it is of use only if there is executional excellence. Unfortunately for us, the project failed as the organisation was unable to implement the tough decisions that were proposed. The organisation needed to demonstrate a resolve and commitment to execute the plan, which it did not.

My learning from that experience was that while a

consultant can propose strategies, at the end of the day, unless the organisation has the leadership in place to execute strategy excellently, nothing happens. For a business, the quality of leadership is exceptionally important and there is often a huge gap between functional leadership and visionary leadership. Ram Charan writes in his best seller book, *Executional Excellence*, that organisations need to ensure that they focus on the execution of their goals. The learning that I took away from that experience is to never take up a job, no matter how financially attractive it is, unless I am sure the organisation has the visionary leadership in place for excellent execution and the management is willing to give a firm commitment to do so.

I learned about the need for executional excellence and I realised my global journey could only be truly satisfying if I executed my plans well. I knew that there would be bumps on the way, but I made up my mind to learn from the problems and move on with my journey. As Steven Covey remarked: 'The main thing is to keep the main thing the main thing.'

The main thing for me, at least at that point, was that I had got started on my global journey finally.

Getting started meant I had to reconfigure myself to fit in to address my shortcomings. Once I gained the confidence, I felt more equipped to get deeper into the world of business and pursue the dreams I set out for myself in this global journey.

*"The main thing is
to keep
the main thing
the main thing."*

Steven Covey

Press Coverage - My coaches always told me press coverage is always good for branding. I guess so, provided the photo looks good and what you say makes sense. One of the stories on corporate couples revealed my full name (Palaniappan Ramanathan Chettiar) instead of my professional name (Palan) and the next morning I was inundated with calls.

Performance
Improvement

VOLUME 46 • NUMBER 4 • APRIL 2007
International Society for Performance Improvement

CONTENTS

Dr Palan rises on power of words

Passion as a trainer inspired him to expand his business empire to include IT and educational institutions

" Like most Indian boys, I was encouraged to be a doctor, lawyer, engineer or some highly-paid professional."

— PALANAPPAN

By LEE KIAN SEONG

TALENT management is essential for all companies, especially for small and medium-scale enterprises (SMEs) order for them to grow their business. However recruiting and retaining talent always hard for SMEs due to their size a lack of emphasis on staff management.

A lot of SMEs view talent management "cost". This need not necessarily be so. T problem is exacerbated when new gene tions are not interested to work in SMEs prefer to join multinational companies.

"This crucial stage of developmental growth often coincides with a period of profit, which explains why proper talent management development is usually not considered by the owners," he says.

In situations where small organisations invest in talent management, the results are surprisingly positive.

"Take the case of the SMR Group, a H-based small HR training and consultancy company of some 32 years. It grew to be an international enterprise and was listed on Bursa Malaysia," he says.

As founder and owner Dr R. Palan believes that talented people play a key role in making the company's culture and business remain "right".

"This was achieved by a long process talent management and intervention to get the better managers and consultants in. Thus there is a need for third or fourth generations of family owners to develop to its full potential, the talent within and releasing the company culture and values to the future development of their business, he says.

Retaining talent

Malaysian Institute of Human Resource Management president Ramley Razali may be difficult for SMEs to secure talent to the general perception that they lac success and therefore lack stability.

Retaining and managing ...key to growth

...ace at the developmental stage

...se within the family. When this is not possible, they employ outsiders.

DATUK DR R. PALAN
CEO
SMR Technologies Bhd

I like the strategic thrust on inculcating Excellence in Human Capital in this budget. I think the budget has focused on a key priority area, human capital, to improve the long-term well-being of the nation and our competitiveness. There are no short-cuts to success.

SBW20 COVER FEATURE   STARBIZWEEK, SATURDAY 9 OCTOBER 2010

By TEE LIN SAY
lintsay@thestar.com.my

Corporate couples

Having a relationship in your business

MARRIED to your job. For quite a few in the country's corporate arena, this rings true in more ways than one. There are many examples of married couples who also manage large corporations as business partners in Malaysia.

In some cases, the co-pilots have together built a thriving business while for others, there have been setbacks from such partnerships.

Some of these business duos in Malaysia, which largely involve family-owned enterprises where husbands and wives are dominant partners include Supermax Corp Bhd's Datuk Seri Stanley Thai and his wife Datin Seri Cheryl Tan, Crest Builder Holdings Bhd's Yong Soon Chow and wife Yoh Hua Lan, Reliance Pacific Bhd's Datuk Gan Eng Kwong and his wife Datin Irene Tan, Freight Management Holdings Bhd's Chew Chong Keat and his wife Gan Siew Yong to name a few.

They are all successful partnerships, but unlike most couples, they face the added and, at times, daunting task of keeping the peace both at home and at work, juggling a meaningful relationship at home with their jet setting careers.

Interestingly though, the principles that apply to these couples both at home and at work do not vary greatly – such as good communication, respect, managing expectations, clearly setting out each other's roles and responsibilities and so forth.

Of course, that's easier said than done, and especially so when it involves millions (or billions) of ringgit.

In such business partnerships, probably ... ...

board, suppliers, customers to shareholders.

Sometimes, one spouse's career can have big repercussions on the other partner's career. For example, the wife sacrifices her plans of taking her MBA because her husband is travelling to and from a foreign country as he is in the middle of implementing a huge overseas contract.

The husband needs somebody he can trust to oversee the operations on a daily basis.

"One of the biggest challenges of working with your partner is that you are not able to see eye to eye on all issues. Sometimes you want a certain risk strategy, and she says no. You must agree to disagree," says SMR Technologies Bhd chairman and CEO Dr Palaniappan Ramanathan Chettiar.

CEO of public relations firm Salina and Associates, Salina Yeop Jr says couples working together can be a bonding factor if both are aligned with a shared objective.

"The challenge is when both parties want to be in the driver's seat or have differing views or values in terms of how the business is managed," she explains.

For example, one party has a risk-averse approach while the other is a risk taker. Another form of challenge comes in the form of the couple wanting to compete with each other rather than complement one another.

Palan says it is important to treat each other ...

Dr Palaniappan Ramanathan Chettiar: 'You must agree to disagree.'

Corporate couples

Company	H...
Autoair Holdings Bhd	Datuk Lie...
Baswell Resources Bhd	Dr Oh Ha...
BHS Industries Bhd	Heng Son...
Crest Builder Holdings Bhd	Yong Soo...
Cymao Holdings Bhd	Lin Tsai-R...
Delloyd Ventures Bhd	Datuk Tee...
DXN Holdings Bhd	Datuk Lim...
DSC Solutions Bhd	Seah Lian...
Engtex Group Bhd	Datuk Ng...
Excel Force MSC Bhd	Wang Ku...
	@ Jeff W...
Freight Management Holdings Bhd	Chew Ch...
I-Bhd	Tan Sri Li...
London Biscuits Bhd	Datuk Se...
Padini Holdings Bhd	Yong Pan...
Reliance Pacific Bhd	Datuk Ga...

SMR Tech shares get thumbs up from TA Sec

September 27 2006

Wednesday 6 October 2010

StarBiz

biz.thestar.com.my

SIDE >> Australia skips interest rate hike >B13

QUOTE OF THE DAY

To make it work, we have to get the implementation and execution right

SMR GROUP CHAIRMAN AND
CEO DR R. PALAN   >B5

BB News

Business Times | 7 March 2006

SMRT shares oversubscribed

Readinglist by **Kathleen Tan** FD@bizedge.com

What are you currently reading?
I am reading the *The McKinsey Mind: Understanding and Implementing the Problem-Solving Tools and Management Techniques of the World's Top Strategic Consulting Firm* by Ethan Rasiel and Paul N Friga at the moment.

**R PALAN, chairman and CEO,
SMR Technologies Bhd**

---

corporate | 18

THEEDGE MALAYSIA

SMR Tech turns the corner

BY Joy Lee

After years of languishing in the red due to an ill-timed entry into the US-ACE Market-listed SMR Technologies Bhd seems to be picking up steam again. Its shift of focus to the Middle Eastern market certainly paid off as the group returned to the black last year with several large projects under its belt.

SMR Tech has secured about 12 projects in the Gulf region worth some RM10 million in over a year, including jobs from Bahrain's Ministry of Works and Abu Dhabi's Ministry of Interior. In the Gulf, the company has a presence in Saudi Arabia, Qatar and the UAE.

RM6.05 million from RM827,000 previously.

It is worth noting that the 1QFY2011 earnings outpaced the company's full-year net profit of RM1.78,000 in FY2010. Assuming it is annualised, the company's net profit could easily exceed RM4.2 million, which works out to a price-earnings ratio of five times. The low PER is consistent with that of ACE Market-listed companies.

But SMR Tech's chairman and CEO Datuk Dr Palaniappan Ramanathan Chettiar is not perturbed by the market not appreciating the improving fundamentals of the company.

He is proud of the fact that the company is getting close to half its revenue from the Middle East.

Palaniappan: After many years, we have discovered the art of winning tenders

In fact, it rose to 61 sen in 2008 before it was adjusted after a bonus issue that was completed at the end of that year.

The company was among the first to experience the impact of the economic downturn in September 2008. It slipped into the red before the actual turmoil hit local shares. It posted a net loss of RM168,000 in 2QFY2008 ended June 30, 2008, compared with a net profit of RM1.98 million a year ago.

SMR Tech had aggressively expanded into the US in late 2007 after its US-based subsidiary signed an agreement to distribute its products there. However, the unexpected global financial crisis forced it to exit the market to cut losses which amounted to RM8 million in 2008.

BRIGHT BUSINESS IDEAS

Training with a local flavour

By Lim Yin Foong

The effectiveness of using passive training aids such as video tapes is often questioned, particularly since many of these videos are imported, and reflect foreign culture and unfamiliar practices to which some Malaysians may not be able to relate.

Not to mention the exorbitant cost of a foreign video (average of RM 2,450) and the fact that the target audience of low-level management may have difficulty understanding the English used in the training videos.

The solution: Create a local training video which Malaysians from all management levels can relate to, and at a much lower cost. After all, the most important thing is to get the message across effectively.

This was the brainwave that training consultancy Specialist Management Resources Sdn Bhd (SMR) came up with when it realised that many Malaysians could not relate culturally and socially to the foreign training videos which the company was importing for Malaysian corporations.

"Even though the ideas or the messages in the tapes were good, many of the target audience did not find some of the practices socially acceptable and therefore were not able to receive the message," says SMR managing director Dr R Palan.

This led to SMR's first locally-produced training video entitled "What the Customer Wants... Just ASK" which uses local talent and concepts to help train front-line service staff on the basics of customer service.

The 17-minute video, which comes with a guide and transparencies for training, is mainly in English but uses Bahasa Malaysia occasionally to make it easier for Malaysians to identify with, says Palan.

The video, which cost RM60,000 to make, was produced by a team of freelance producers and actors put together by SMR four months ago. According to Palan, the local production costs 50 per cent cheaper than that of a foreign video, yet achieves 80 per cent of the technical standards of those found in a foreign video.

Response to the RM1,000-price tag video since its launch in late November has been good, he says, with 28 tapes sold to date. The video, which Palan says can be used by all companies, has so far been purchased by mainly large service-oriented companies.

Despite the Malaysian market for training videos being relatively small, SMR has ambitious plans for its locally-produced videos. It plans to produce another six videos in 1995, says Palan. In the pipeline are two videos which will deal with supervision and with telephone skills.

"We anticipate annual sales of 100 copies for each video," he adds confidently.

Given the small Malaysian market, SMR also plans to distribute its Malaysian-made training videos to neighbouring countries like Singapore, Brunei and Indonesia whose citizens, Palan feels, would be able to relate to the video.

"Video is a go-between medium, to help ease people into more technology-based learning," he states.

Having moved into new learning technologies two years ago, SMR has also been exploring other methods of technology-based learning such as utilising the computer with CD-ROMs and interactive discs.

Palan reveals that SMR's next

Palan: Video is a go-between medium

step is to put its locally-produced videos into CD-ROM format. Its first CD-ROM training programme is expected to be ready by April 1995, and will be sold at 40 per cent of the price of an imported CD-ROM training programme.

He says the company will also look into producing its own training modules in the more costly interactive discs.

"The trend is moving away from face-to-face learning to more technology-based learning,

although it will take a while for Malaysia to switch over," Palan predicts, adding that at present, only five per cent of Malaysian companies are using more learning techniques while the rest still stick to traditional face-to-face training which provide the coaching and mentoring that the more passive video lacks.

He however feels that as one enters the information age, these technology-based techniques are needed especially if one has a huge group to train.

APPOINT

Make a rainbow make a change

By S. Jai Shankar

THE rainbow is a beautiful phenomenon. To the young, it is awe inspiring. To the adult, it is a manifestation of nature's grandeur.

But to R. Palan, the rainbow symbolises the nature of life – the colours and hues of a rainbow represent the full range of life's intricacies.

Using rainbow as an analogy, Palan develops ideas and pointers which he hopes will hand his readers the beacon of understanding to better handle the pressures of the modern world.

However, the ideas in this book are not original.

This is something that Palan, much to his credit, freely acknowledges in the very first chapter.

What he has done is take strains of related ideas from different authorities, and integrate them with his personal experiences to produce

Book 2 Read — This column features current books on various business issues. This week, we feature a book that looks into having a balanced life.

a montage of well reasoned advice and opinions.

It is difficult to categorise this book. It is a cross between a self-help book and a book on leadership.

Maybe this is not surprising considering the fact that the author is a trained professional speaker and a human resources development consultant (he is also the chairperson of Specialist Management Resources Sdn Bhd).

Throughout the book, Palan stresses the need for readers to create their own rainbows.

Our rainbows, he writes, should have these seven components – the ability to make a difference; ability to

embrace change; determination; self image and self suggestions; desire and enthusiasm; leadership and adventure; and finally love and encouragement.

He notes that to build the personal rainbow, one would require to have many positive qualities.

For example, Palan writes that individuals must have a stable emotional quotient (EQ) to succeed in their career. He points out that individuals lacking in emotional stability might ruin themselves.

For example, he states, displaced anger can subvert a friendship or disturb office harmony.

Thus, it needs to be

checked and controlled and this can only be done with proper emotional control.

He also touches on the need to have a balanced life-style, between work and personal life. He offers many real-life anecdotes, usually culled from past experience, and personal knowledge, to clarify this position.

Palan advises his readers to evaluate their life priorities and examine whether there is a necessity to reinvent themselves. Hence, although, having a balanced lifestyle is usually seen as a cliche, the author, a firm believer of balanced living, urges the readers to practise it. Palan's writing is very personal and this makes his message resonate very strongly.

His emotive writing style ensures his words tweak your emotions and common sense at the turn of every page, very much so when he speaks about something personal.

LIFETIME ACHIEVEMENT: Taib (second right) receives a crystal trophy from Palan (left) and Sheikh Fadzir as Dr Chan applauds.

Coverage by the Sarawak press

CHAPTER 3

Differentiation

. . .

I t is said, "Don't compete, just make competition irrelevant" by offering something that competitors don't. By this stage, I had been to several developed countries and in all of these economies, one of the things I noticed in the business of training was that people used brands to differentiate themselves from the crowd. Marketers of course understand the importance of branding. So do leading professional service firms, but not many entrepreneurs understand the significance of branding.

In the training and consulting industry, particularly in businesses that are not self-regulated, you find a plethora of consultants. They have either retired or been displaced from their jobs. In a profession with a low entry barrier, it is easy to get started but difficult to sustain a profitable business, particularly when you do not stand out from the crowd.

Erin Casey, writing in the *Success* magazine, says that to succeed in an overcrowded, hypercompetitive world, you have to make an impression on your customers by breaking through the noise. Lauron Sonnier, in *Think Like a Marketer*, says that just telling people how great you are, your product is or how affordable you are is not good enough. Four questions need to be addressed to stand out in a competitive world:

1. What do I want?
2. How do I want to be perceived in the market place?
3. Who is my customer?
4. How do I define success now and in the future?

In fact, all of us stand out in some way as we leave impressions behind with those we meet and interact with. Even today, when I am much more of a professional manager, customers see me more as a FUN trainer. When I ask my family about how they perceive me, they say 'serious'. If you ask your friends and family about how they see you, they surely would have an adjective to describe you. Steve Jobs and Apple are famous for their iconic 'Think Different' campaign. Apple is recognised not just as a better computer or a better company, but as one that is different. It stands out from other computers and organisations. Their products are cool and exceptionally user friendly. Four things can differentiate us from others.

1. **Do different things:** You stand out in the crowded place when you are unique. You are doing what no

one else is doing. Take the example of John Cleese, the actor trainer extraordinaire who pioneered Video Arts training videos that are crazily funny.

2. **Do things differently:** You show your customers that the 'how' can be more important than the 'what'. In my experience, I think Singapore Airlines, a full service airline, makes flying a great experience. They treat every passenger as special. On the other hand, Air Asia, a low cost airline has made flying affordable for most people even if it is not a full service airline. Both of them do things differently but in line with their business goals.

3. **Do things with contagious enthusiasm:** Make your customers enjoy the experience and get them to be enthusiastic about you, your product and your service. Make them feel emotional about the product. Make them happy. Zig Ziglar, the world class speaker had this to say: "People don't buy for logical reasons. They buy for emotional reasons."

4. **Do things consistently:** We can only stand out if we do all the above three consistently. The image sticks and we create an identity that people can relate to and trust. A brand promise works only when the promise is delivered. An investor and

trusted friend, Ed Jackson, always had this to say: "Palan, the product must do all the time what you say it will do."

Differentiation starts with asking your close family, friends and customers how they perceive you. Would their perception match with yours? The market in which you operate must see the value you offer. They must use appropriate adjectives that describe you, your company, product, service, staff, processes, policies, office – in short, everything. Each one of us has to make an official attributes list and find out if we are making the right impressions. Success happens when the business stands out not just in a good way, but also the right way.

In my early days as a training professional, I found myself doing a variety of things. In fact, people would describe me as a generalist rather than a specialist trainer. It was my colleague and friend, Dr. Nat, who insisted on the need to develop a niche product or service.

The first lesson learned was the need to *learn by observing role models and brand leaders* in the market place. When I went to the US, Bob Pike had the Instructor Led Participative Training Tools brand, Ed Scannel had his Games Trainers Play and Alan Pease, Body Language. There were Asians too who had built a brand for themselves, such as Ken Blanchatd (Leadership Management), Richard Chan

*"People don't buy
for logical reasons.
They buy
for emotional reasons."*

Zig Ziglar

(Quality) and Thiagi (Frame Games & Small Groups) in the U.S., Swami Parthasarathy (Life discourses) in India, Lawrence Chan (Motivation) in Malaysia and many others. I observed the masters in the training industry who had differentiated themselves from the market. They stood out in the training industry by doing things that were unique. They were very clear in what they wanted, who their customers were and how they wanted to be perceived in the market. Their inclination was not just to become rich but also to go further. They wanted to deliver value to their customers. This observation led me to reflect on what it is that I wanted.

I was now able to see the need to differentiate myself from the market. I had long wanted adults to learn in an effective way. My goal had always been to make learning exciting and easy by cutting down the learning curve. I started experimenting with FUN tools to make learning effective. I didn't want to be seen as a generalist trainer who ran every other programme. I started setting for myself a differentiation policy, whereby I would turn down jobs that did not relate to the key areas that I wanted to be known for. So in the late 80's I would've done a time management programme but in the late 90's I didn't want to focus on that. I told myself that my market will primarily consist of trainers, HR professionals, and business leaders at the middle management level. I was still growing in experience and I was aware that to train top management, you needed a certain age and experience profile. So, that was not my priority at that time.

The second lesson learned was the importance of ***doing different things and doing things differently***. While it was important to be noticed as an Asian train-the-trainer specialist, I also had to do things differently. I started dabbling with creative tools with the help of my colleagues Dr. Nat and Dr. Ramanathan. With their help, I came up with the model FUN x CONTENT = RESULTS. We were able to conclude that FUN is a vehicle to deliver content for *The Magic of Making Training FUN!!*, with its unique training tools and style of delivery. I believed that content is a required condition, no doubt, but FUN is going to be the facilitating factor. It was not always explicit in my mind that I wanted my training to be fun, but certainly all along I'd used FUN tools in my journey.

I found that a trainer's ability to engage his audience sets him apart from others. It is important to deliver needs based training that is engaging and perceived by the learners as useful to them. There is no way you can force people to use something they see no value in and a trainer only adds value when participants use what they have learned back at the workplace.

Now, in my search for a distinct training programme with a unique style of training, I was able to validate my own experiences. I was able to tell myself: "There must be something in FUN learning tools. If participants are engaged and they like the content, then there must be something I'm doing to add value."

The third lesson learned was that **contagious enthusiasm** was essential for differentiation. When we designed the FUN training style and used FUN learning tools, we did that passionately. It was not about sales or revenue but it was all about getting enthusiastic in helping people learn so that they may achieve their performance goals. It is the contagious enthusiasm that gets you started and sustains your journey.

We took pains to explain that FUN is not being funny. It is a tool that facilitates a purposeful learning experience, which is enjoyable at the same time. So we gave people a framework which allows for a lot of flexibility within the structure. The goal was not to be prescriptive with a one-size-fits-all model, but to recognise the different learning styles and cultural diversity.

Back to work applications were important to me. Participants received frame games, frame humour, frame quotes where they could plug in relevant content. Participants went back to their workplaces and used some of the FUN tools and called to tell us about the difference the tools made to them personally and professionally. It meant that FUN tools actually improved learner retention and motivation.

This is an instance of the egg cracking moment I was talking about earlier. It is easy to think that *The Magic of Making Training FUN!!* actually happened overnight. It didn't – it just brought together in one place what I had been practising over a period of 12 years. Now we had a Unique Selling Point. We had a different product that was delivered differently to adult learners who wanted to help others learn effectively.

The fourth lesson learned was the need to be **consistent in focus and follow through,** doing what you think is important for the brand, all the time. In logic, it is said, consistency is achieved when there is no contradiction. Consistency reinforces the image you are hoping to create in the marketplace. It is living the brand on a daily basis. I have seen world renowned comedians being on show every minute. They live the brand with sheer consistency. Additionally, consistency also makes you better in what you do. There is a saying that your game only gets as good as your practice. Doing it again and again in a consistent manner not only reinforces your brand but also helps you get better in what you do. Again, beware of getting into the trap of assuming that consistency means there is no need for innovation.

While consistency builds brands, one of the difficulties in making the brand endure globally is the challenge to be relevant in markets differentiated by variables such as culture. While we have to be consistent, we also need to change with changing customer needs and times to stay relevant. Differentiation and brand building requires consistency as well as the ability to innovate to meet your customer's expectations when things change on the ground. A blogger, Christine Arden, refers to this alchemy as the art of being "consistently surprising." This is a great idea but let me tell you from my experience it is never easy. It is about being flexible in meeting the customers' needs while staying true to your core ideas and principles. Thus, FUN training remains the core idea but in its implementation, an off-the-shelf training game from an earlier time can now be replaced with an online training game to engage Gen Z learners.

The fifth lesson learned was the need to **communicate your differentiation to your customers.** We never run a programme without FUN tools even if that means getting stereotyped as fun trainers. To me that is acceptable because we want to be known as the fun trainers. It is just that we have to evolve and move beyond being predictable. Your website, Facebook or Tweets need to reflect your differentiation. How are you different from others? We went through that process in developing the tools needed to demonstrate our passion in FUN training.

Ultimately, when you are different and you add value to your customers, your business moves up the value chain. The differentiation has to be good for your customers and it has to be right for you in that it adds value to your business.

Humbled with the award from His Royal Highness Sultan Azlan Shah on the occasion of His Royal Highness' birthday on April 19, 2011. Conferred the DPMP award carrying the title of Dato'.

Awarded the Certified Speaking Professional (CSP) Award, the highest earned award for professional speakers, from the President Kristin Arnold, National Speakers Association of USA. Another significant step in the world of professional speaking.

Conferred the Fellowship by Mike Long of the British Institute of Learning & Development, UK, another step forward in the world of learning and development.

Receiving the Malaysian Institute of Human Resources Management Award (MIHRM) in 2007 from His Excellency, the Honourable Prime Minister of Malaysia, Dato' Seri Najib Abdul Razak.

Second placing for the company at the Enterprise 50 Awards organised by the Ministry of International Trade & Industry., Malaysia. With Her Excellency, the then Minister, Tan Sri Rafidah Aziz.

Honoured with the 17th placing award at the Hong Kong 2005 Asia Pacific Deloittes Technology Fast 500.

Growth is about partnerships. On the occasion of signing the MOU in 2006 with PPM Indonesia in the presence of His Excellency Tun Dr Mahathir Mohamad, former Prime Minister of Malaysia.

The Gulf Cooperation Council (GCC) countries are great growth economies. With Her Excellency Sheikha Lubna bint Khalid bin Sultan Al Qasimi, the then Minister for Foreign Trade, United Arab Emirates (UAE).

With the inspirational and legendary Tan Sri Tony Fernandez, the man who defied the odds and created thousands of jobs. A perfect outsider who showed the world 'if I can do it, anyone with the concept and belief can achieve it'. The founder of Air Asia, Tune Hotels, Tune Talk, Tune Insurance and the owner of QPR Football Club.

2005 Asia HRD Congress, Kuala Lumpur. With His Excellency, the then Minister of Human Resources, Malaysia, Tan Sri Dr. Fong Chan Onn.

2008 Asia HRD Congress, Jakarta. With His Excellency Jusuf Kalla, the Vice President of Indonesia and Chairman of PPM Indonesia.

With His Excellency, the former Deputy Prime Minister of India Shri L.K. Advani, in Hong Kong.

With Dr Goh, Senior Manager, Cabin Crew Training, Singapore Airlines and Her Excellency Datin Paduka Seri Rosmah Mansor, wife of the Honourable Prime Minister of Malaysia at the Asia HRD Awards.

The SMR English Language Mentors with His Excellency the Deputy Prime Minister of Malaysia, Tan Sri Muhyiddin bin Yassin.

The Asia HRD Awards Bahrain – Dr Ibrahim El Dossary, Prime Minister's Court, Kingdom of Bahrain presenting the Award to His Excellency Dr. Abdul-Hussain bin Ali Mirza, Minister of Energy, Bahrain. Also in picture Origin Group Ahmad Albanna and the President of Bahrain Society of Training & Development.

With the celebrated author and speaker Brian Tracy, a role model for writers like me.

Being the Chair of the Working Committee on HRD, ASEAN Chamber of Commerce & Industry was a unique experience.

At the Taiwan Bankers Club, on sidelines of the 1992 World Conference on Training with two stalwarts in the world of Human Resources: Professor Don Kirkpatrick and George Webster, Executive Director of the Institute of Training & Development, U.K.

With world famous Ken Blanchard, author of One Minute Manager

A chance photo opportunity with the renowned Peter Yarrow, the American singer who found fame with the 1960s folk music trio Peter, Paul and Mary, on the sidelines of the Orlando American Society of Training & Development, 1990.

AUSLIG, one of our early Australian customers for our software HRDPower. In picture, Gabriel Nyeholt, then our Australian colleague.

HRDPower team at the conclusion of the implementation project with the senior management of National Drilling Company, U.A.E.-

CHAPTER 4

Growth

. . .

As a concept, growth is an incredible term, complex to understand. While growth is often seen in economic terms, it is much more. It can be economic, social or personal. No matter how people approach the concept of growth, there is general agreement that it is an essential ingredient for progress. Individuals and businesses experience various stages of growth. The much acclaimed playwright William Shakespeare, in his play *As You Like It*, compares the world to a stage and life to a play where everyone passes through seven stages of growth from infancy to old age. Similarly, businesses also go through different stages of growth: start up, growth, maturity and decline.

In the context of a person's career, it is often said that if you do not move forwards, you are moving backwards. What does moving forward involve? It involves growing your own personal competence to move up the career ladder. The *Harvard Business Review*, in an article on management tips, outlines the need for every person to take responsibility for their own growth. Growth as the development of personal competence is highlighted by Stewart Johnson who said, "Our business in life is not to get ahead of others, but to get ahead of ourselves – to break our own records, to outstrip our yesterday by our today."

Some success stories leave you speechless, particularly when the stories are about entrepreneurs who started from scratch. In business, take the example of an outsider to the aviation business, Tony Fernandez – born in Malaysia, educated in the UK and employed for the most part in the music industry before he ventured into aviation. In 2001, he took over a fledgling airline that was about to go out of business and within 10 years he built it into a billion dollar corporation with over 100 planes and 10,000 people. Today, his company Tune Group operates hotels, financial services and mobile networks in Malaysia. Tony Fernandez owns the English football club QPR and has interests in Formula One racing. With fellow shareholders, Fernandez bought over British sports car maker Caterham in 2012. He also co-owns a prestigious London club with pop star Madonna.

Okay, that sort of success is one in a million, some may say. Let me give you another example. In 1987, my wife and I

*"Our business in life is not
to get ahead of others,
but to get ahead
of ourselves-to
break our own records,
to outstrip our yesterday
by our today."*

Stewart Johnson

moved to the residential district of Bangsar in Kuala Lumpur. Every evening we would eat out and one of our favourite eating places was a small roadside shop that sold chapattis and rotis. The roadside stall was owned by a Malaysian Indian lady. She had no access to easy credit nor was she connected to any politician or industrialist. She was one among the millions who aspire to make some money and ensure that the next generation can have a better life than theirs. Probably her daily sales at that point would have been about 200 Ringgit Malaysia. Within a few years, she managed to convert the roadside stall into a small shop and by 2002 she had a restaurant franchise with sales touching a million ringgit a month. Today she runs many restaurants under her franchise in Kuala Lumpur.

In arts, there are numerous success stories. I would like to cite some personal favourites. Take the example of Meryl Streep, who grew into one of the most accomplished actresses of all time. In a career spanning over three decades, she won accolades for a variety of performances right from her 1977 film *Julia* to the one of the latest, *The Iron Lady*, where she portrays the role of Margaret Thatcher. There are countless others: Indian actor Kamal Haasan, Hong Kong star Jackie Chan, Malaysian actor Michelle Yeoh and Indian violinist L. Subramaniam, to cite a few. They grew into great performers as a result of learning from their experiences. Knowledge management, observing other experts, and experimenting with fusion music and new film technologies led to their personal and professional growth. Coupled with talent, their tremendous effort resulted in stardom. They invested "10,000 hour" honing their talent and skills. The idea of "10,000 Hour Rule" popularised by Malcolm Gladwell and based on a study by Anders Ericsson simply states that success requires an investment of enormous time. While Gladwell is often criticised as a pop economist, his ideas certainly made sense to me. The notion that success can be achieved by working on your specific skills 20 hours every week for 10 years made perfect sense to me. They did not start out as great artistes, but grew into world class professionals with deliberate pratice in their fields.

Muhammad Yunus, Nobel Prize winner and the founder of Grameen Bank, pioneered and developed the concepts of microcredit and microfinance. A Professor of Economics, he showed the world how to empower the poor through loans that are given to entrepreneurs too poor to qualify for traditional bank loans. In 2006, Yunus and his Grameen Bank received the Nobel Peace Prize "for their efforts through microcredit to create economic and social development from below." He created a tipping point in the world. Microcredit and microfinance has grown exponentially to address social imbalances. It was estimated a few years ago that over 70 million people have received microcredit totalling about 38 billion US dollars. Repayment rates are about 95 to 98%. Yunus was able to effect the tipping point. Gladwell in his book *The Tipping Point: How Little Things Can Make a Big Difference* defines it as the moment of critical mass, the threshold, the boiling point, when a huge change happens suddenly and unexpectedly.

My first lesson in understanding growth as a business, professional or personal concept was the need for *clarity in thinking*. Many of my mentors and friends like Dr. Nat and Ed Jackson have asked me this question countless number of times to the point of irritating me – "What is it that you want?" The answers I gave them did not reflect what I really wanted. I was never able to answer the question clearly, though clarity in thinking is often the first step necessary for growth. In my own way, I always wanted to grow – personally, as a mature person, professionally, as a competent HR professional who is able to compete with the world's best and financially, as someone with a good quality of life. I wanted to work with different audiences on unique and original areas.

My journey into the world of training, speaking and business started when I was a student doing my Masters in 1978. The Christian Conference of Asia, a non-governmental organisation, gave me an opportunity to conduct a few sessions in a youth training programme. This was my first paid job even though the fee that I received for that assignment is negligible. I guess the reason I was given the opportunity was because the confirmed trainer could not make it at the last minute. Training the young people was a good break for me in the field of learning, besides being a chance to earn some money. Subsequently, with some of my classmates, we formed a youth organisation called REACH and organised a national event that was funded by corporate sponsors. Again, this was a great opportunity to learn about so many things such as organising, speaker management, VIP protocols, banquet arrangements and media relations.

Many years later, working as a part-time trainer with the Malaysian franchise of the Institute of Supervisory Management, UK and the Association of Business Executives allowed me to interact with working adults. While training working adults, I learned that their expectations were much higher. They wanted skills and knowledge that grew their careers.

Around this time, I thought I had the training and speaking competence to start a business. Little did I realise that being good in training or speaking did not necessarily mean you can succeed in business. Being business savvy or having a business mindset is very different from just delivering a training programme. The first business I started nearly made me go broke. With a little bit of luck and support from friends, I hit pay dirt with some successful conferences. Then I sold the company to an acquaintance for a paltry sum to open another boutique firm that had no identity. Eventually these two experiences gave me the clarity that was essential to grow a business and resulted in me starting my present company. The need to systematically move between Kiyosaki's quadrants: E, S, B and I is an important one for growing up. I was very clear that I wanted to start a professional services firm with a growth trajectory. Now that I had a vision, I could aspire to grow. Having a clear goal was not enough. I realised the importance of demonstrating leadership qualities in order to succeed. As Jack Welch said: "Good business leaders create a vision, articulate the vision, passionately own the vision, and relentlessly drive it to completion."

The second lesson that I learned in my journey as a professional in business is the need to **evolve and change as the markets evolve**. Leo Tolstoy remarked that everyone thinks of changing the world but no one thinks of changing himself. Without the ability to change with changing times, growth will remain a futile concept. In my own journey, I have had to let go of obsolete concepts, products and emotional baggage.

I recognised the need to evolve with changing times to stay relevant both personally and professionally. The concept of training was undergoing a change. Training was seen as something that was imposed upon people and therefore, there was a movement to differentiate training from learning. All of a sudden organisations renamed their training officers as 'learning officers.' Even though it looked like semantics to me, I could not ignore what was happening out there in the world. Whether you call it 'training' or 'learning', at the end of the day, it was an activity aimed at bringing about learning. Unfortunately, the market perception was that training was an imposed change.

*"Good business leaders
create a vision,
articulate the vision,
passionately own the vision,
and relentlessly drive it
to completion."*

Jack Welch

At that point in time, we used to organise a hugely successful event called Trainers Meet Trainers. The event had grown over the years into a large one that provided us tremendous brand leverage. When the concept of training changed, it was obvious that organisations looked at development as something broader than what could be achieved by training. It was clear that Trainers Meet Trainers as a product was no longer relevant in the market in the current form. Psychologist Viktor Frankl said, "When we are no longer able to change the situation, we are challenged to change ourselves." The idea to develop a new product called Asia HRD Congress was pushed by colleagues like Dr. Nat and Khiem. With the launch of Asia HRD Congress, we were able to recapture the momentum and grow the events business once again. Today Asia HRD Congress has grown into a quality event.

The third lesson in my journey to understand growth was the need to *create communities of practice*. Etienne Wenger, a social learning theorist known for his work on communities of practices, tried to understand the connection between knowledge, community, learning and identity. He contended that human knowing is fundamentally a social act and this has profound implications for the way we think and attempt to help people learn. From a business and learning perspective, I concurred with his views and began to see the need for learning to be interconnected. I could also recognise the networking power of communities.

*"When we are
no longer able
to change the situation,
we are challenged to
change ourselves."*

Viktor Frankl

There is the famous Six Degrees of Separation theory, unproven but popular, which postulates that one person can be connected to another through a chain that has no more than five intermediaries. The 'chains' theory, first proposed by Hungarian Frigyes Karinthy, was recently popularised by Seth Godin author of the book *Six Pixels of Separation* and Mitch Joel, author of *Ctrl Alt Delete*. It is all about networking to grow in a very competitive world. Mitch Joel's blog is inspiring for all of us who want to be networked via the social media. His book offers important lessons for those who want to take advantage of the social media revolution and stay connected with one another. As his book reviewer says, "Is it important to be connected? Well, consider this: If Facebook were a country, it would have the sixth largest population in the world. The truth is that we no longer live in a world of six degrees of separation. In fact, we're now down to only six pixels of separation, which changes everything we know about doing business." Technology, marketing, networking, branding and entrepreneurship have converged in a practical way.

Today, a community of practice is essential for the growth of a business. Apple is a company that has successfully built a community that fuels its business. I have been an ardent Apple fan for years, like many of the millions who are die-hard supporters. If you are a LinkedIn (www.linkedin.com) member, you can visualise the power of connections. Malcolm Gladwell in his best seller book *The Tipping Point* refers to connectors. Connectors know a lot of people and help to bring people together in social circles.

The *Harvard Business Review* (HBR) guide to networking provides tools and advice on networking selectively or thematically, based on a core purpose. It covers six vital areas:

1. create and maintain the right ties in a way that feels authentic;
2. nourish relationships through give and take;
3. share—and spread—ideas;
4. use social media tools to network;
5. manage your image online; and
6. reach out after losing touch.

Long before the advent of the internet, I learned from my mentors that the key to growth was in the ability to connect with people. Even in those early days, we were ardent followers of the ACT Contact Management software system that helped us connect with people. I learned from British trainers Richard Story and David Greenberg about the need to remember faces and names.

My team and I aspired to build communities in the markets we served for our professional development and the sustainable growth of the business. We built a FUN practice for Learning and Development professionals. The use of FUN tools provided us with a distinctive style to help people learn faster and far more effectively in terms of retention. This resulted in better transfer of learning to the workplace. There is a saying in the professional services industry that all you need is an optimum number of customers for success. You need to delight them with your service to keep them. The larger the community, the easier it is to grow the business.

Realising the importance of communities, the Trainers Meet Trainers and Asia HRD Congress events were designed as distinctive platforms for interaction among human resources development professionals. The concept behind these events was to give every trainer – competitor or not – a spot in the limelight on the simple philosophy that the world is full of opportunities. We wanted to start with a surplus mentality instead of seeing the market as a place of diminished opportunities. Our purpose was to make the cake bigger for everyone on the premise, "I am not going to take anything away from you. You are not going to take anything away from me." We have worked on building this community for close to three decades and believe we have left a footprint in the industry.

The fourth lesson in my quest for growth was to *think differently*. I really wanted the business to grow. I do not have a story to bowl you over, but may be a story to share my own experiences with you. At that point of time, I saw growth not in terms of quantum leaps but really as a modest movement forward in both revenue and profitability. I soon realised that when people talk about growth in the corporate world, they are not talking about a small boutique firm doing a few million dollars. They are talking about growth in quantum leaps that completely changes the way the game is played.

Dell changed the way personal computers were sold, Microsoft made computing so easy, the internet changed the way we worked, Google transformed our lives with an enormous ability to search for anything in this world with a click, Facebook showed us how we can connect with one another, the mobile phone revolutionised the world of communications, low cost travel made it affordable for everyone to fly, Amazon changed the face of retailing and the iPad and the iPhone changed the IT industry. They were all led by thought leaders who dared to think differently on a mega scale but there are many other success stories that are not this snazzy or huge. One such simple success story is that of William Berry.

William Berry is a successful entrepreneur who divides his time between three cities running diverse businesses. One of his ventures, *Accommodation for Students*, is an online portal for students seeking accommodation. He started the venture with co-founder Simon Thompson in 2000 after graduating from Manchester Metropolitan University, where Berry was apparently voted peer most likely to make a million. His biggest focus is on customer service, which he describes as key to the survival of a business. His role model is Tony Hsieh, the founder of Zappos. Tony sold his delivery company to Amazon for a whopping 1.2 billion US dollars in 2009. Hsieh wrote the best seller book *Delivering Happiness: A Path to Profits, Passion, and Purpose*. Hsieh's goal is to stun customers with stunning customer service – his number one value being 'Deliver WOW Through Service.'

Reflecting on economic and business growth taught me two terms: 'non-linearity' and 'scalability.' Non-linear and scalable businesses give entrepreneurs financial freedom and independence, but it also requires them to think differently.

In my journey, we tried to think differently. The event Trainers Meet Trainers was followed by the book *The Magic of Making Training FUN!!* and in a small way, they were successful initiatives that provided the organisation with the financial freedom to pursue things that mattered to us. The organisation was certainly growing, but one of the biggest challenges was that the business, whether training or consulting, wasn't scalable or non-linear. Of course we started writing books in order to create intellectual property, but books priced at around 39.90 Ringgit Malaysia could not be considered the vehicle for huge growth because we just couldn't get the mass. Certainly, the books helped us position the organisation and create intellectual property. There was professional growth, but we could not experience any economic growth. There was a need to leapfrog in our thinking to achieve our goals.

Thus as the world was caught up in the Y2K problem towards the end of 1999, we were looking for opportunities for growth in the form of scalable products that were non-linear. We had to think out-of-the-box – a cliché phrase used by most trainers and consultants, but a powerful one indeed in the everyday world of business.

One thing that struck me was the need for a user-friendly and affordable software system. As we looked around, we found that there were tonnes of HR software out there. There were mainly three types: tier one products consisting of large enterprise systems such as Oracle (PeopleSoft) and SAP, tier two products that were specialised applications and tier three products consisting of transactional type of more affordable HR software such as payroll products. We identified a niche in the tier two category.

Several new developments were taking place in the market. Business Process Outsourcing was gaining strength and thought leaders were talking about the need for a strategic HR management tool. With McKinsey talking about the War for Talent, the emphasis was shifting towards specialised applications in Talent Management, Succession Planning and Competency Management.

Around this time, the competency management movement was gaining momentum in Australia and the UK.

With governments focusing on job creation, many countries started embarking on the National Vocational Qualification framework to create a skilled workforce. There is a Chinese saying that when the winds of change blow, some people build walls and others build windmills. Our windmill creation led us to focus on a niche – application: competency management to address the need to develop, assess and manage competencies. That took me to Perth, Australia, as that was close to Malaysia and on the same time zone. We started working with a software developer. When we started down the technology road, we were clear that we wanted to do HR software because that was where our strength was. We did not want to do supply chain, body shopping or financial management. It is like wanting to drive a car. You don't want to manufacture cars or be in the car parts business. You just want to drive. Similarly, we just wanted to do people management using competency tools.

The competency management software was an extension of what we knew, but it incurred new learning. While we knew HR and training, we were not necessarily software experts. I always remember the saying that if we are to discover new oceans, we must have the courage to lose sight of the shore. We also had to establish the thought leadership for young developers to code what we wanted the software to do.

For example, a software programmer would want to create a calendar application which would take two programmers about 20 days of work, costing us approximately 8000 to 10,000 US dollars. But instead of developing it in-house we realised we could go over to components.com and buy a calendar application for just 30 US dollars and integrate it with our product. We had to keep our focus on the fact that we were trying to develop a competency based application, not trying to sell a calendar application.

We had to make business choices. For instance, we found that it was far more expensive to write a line of code in Australia than it is in India or Malaysia. On the other hand, the quality of work and the rigorous testing was better in Australia. Eventually, we decided to get back to Malaysia. I'd like to make a point about the key skills of scanning and observation in business. Many entrepreneurs wait for an opportunity, only to miss them right under their noses. In 1998, the Malaysian government launched the Multimedia Super Corridor programme which changed business operations dramatically. It offered investors several incentives including a ten year tax break. Also, we could get a software expert from any part of the world within eight days to work at Cyberjaya, Malaysia. In our case, we got developers primarily from India and they were supported by experts from other locations. We thus had the best of both worlds – quality workforce and the cost efficiencies of working in Malaysia.

Finally, we had a product which did reasonably well. The software gave us a huge opportunity in that now we did not necessarily have to be in front of the customer as trainers and consultants to generate revenue. We could actually create a product and deploy it across multiple locations. Finally we had found a product that was scalable and non-linear. However, marketing a software product was completely different from what we used to do. We soon realised that going into the training room and delivering a programme or entering into a consulting engagement was different from providing a software to a client.

We recognised that we needed to continually improve to keep pace with technology. To add value to a customer, we had to be alert to customer requirements. Early on, we decided that we would not chase technology or follow every trend that appeared in the market, but we would be technology-led so that we wouldn't go obsolete. We worked with Microsoft.Net frameworks.

It also meant that I had to go back to school and learn business terms and concepts new to me. I grappled with financial terms like 'amortisation' and 'depreciation' because to succeed I had to be not just technologically up-to-date, but financially savvy too. You realise that you have invested a million dollars in a product and your auditor says that it has to be amortised over a period of 5 years from the day you commercialised the product. And if you overinvested in your research and development (R & D), you are in trouble. If you did not finish your product on time, you are in trouble. If you did finish your product on time, then you have to get your pricing right and also sell enough to make money. Yes, the business had turned scalable and non-linear, yet this leg of the journey wasn't as easy as it sounded. 'Scalable', 'Non-Linear' and 'High Growth' are seducing terms but can be fatal attractions if one is not careful.

Clarity in thinking is essential but so is thinking differently. The future of any company lies not only in evolving to meet customer needs but also in appreciating that it can be done differently. Are we an HR company? Are we a technology company? Are we in education services? The answer is not a black and white one. What we are doing is meeting the needs of the customer in the learning and performance space and that is how we like to see ourselves, we are crafting a Learning Hub strategy. A few years ago we had a vision statement that said we wanted to partner with organisations to develop their employee potential. We wanted to be the partner of choice to help organisations realise their employee potential. It still holds, it is just that we have expanded to enable people to realise their potential. We want to help create value and our contribution will be in the learning and performance space, where our core strength rests.

As most creativity experts say, we think we know it all when we become adults but what we all experience is the narrowing of the imagination. Growth requires that we think differently. Einstein remarked: "We cannot solve our problems with the same thinking we used when we created them."

The fifth lesson in my global journey about growing the business is about *ensuring that the business is growing profitably yet in a sustainable way.* In a world where organisations are being measured by quarterly earnings, a focus on growth and a balanced approach in managing costs is necessary. An emphasis on growth alone cannot lead us on the path to success. We need to ensure that people and organisations have the capabilities to execute the business strategies for sustained profitable growth. We have to ensure capability within the organisation.

Successful organisations such as Toyota or the Dabbawallas in India may be worlds apart when we consider a systems perspective but both have a growth oriented culture. Every employee understands what is meant by growth, whether it is in terms of sales volume, market share, profitability, high margins or market leadership. Growth can also be dangerous if there is a lack of planning. Sales may be discounting sales and long term gains can be destroyed with short term approaches. We need to have in place the tools to measure what we mean

*"We cannot
solve our problems
with the same thinking
we used when
we created them."*

Albert Einstein

by growth. There has to be an intense focus on acquiring the human capabilities to execute growth plans and strategies.

I had a difficult conversation with a colleague who was nervous about hiring people smarter than he. It took all of my communications skills to explain that we are better off having people smarter than us rather than those who are less smart than us. The founder of Aditya Birla Group was said to have impressed upon all his family members the need to hire people smarter than themselves in order to grow and build the business. Today Aditya Birla Group is a Fortune 500 company, a 40 billion US dollar corporation. It is anchored by an extraordinary force of over 136,000 employees belonging to 42 different nationalities. The Group was ranked No.4 globally and No.1 in Asia Pacific in the 'Top Companies for Leaders' survey, 2011.

Jack Welch remarked: "I was never the smartest guy in the room. From the first person I hired, I was never the smartest guy in the room. And that's a big deal. And if you're going to be a leader – if you're a leader and you're the smartest guy in the world–in the room, you've got real problems."

In my global journey as an entrepreneur, I have learned that growth is mandatory. We do not have a choice. Standing still is not an option. It is often said there is no such thing as work-life balance; there are only work-life choices, and

"I was never the smartest guy in the room.
From the first person I hired, I was never the smartest guy in the room.
And that's a big deal.
And if you're going to be a leader-if you're a leader and you're the smartest guy in the world-in the room, you've got real problems."

Jack Welch

whatever choices you make have consequences. That is what I have realised in my transition from a solo entrepreneur to leading a public listed corporation today.

1997, my first book "The Magic of Making Training FUN!!", launched by Capt Mohd Kamil Abu Bakar, Director of Training, Malaysian Airlines.

1998, His Excellency Tan Sri Abdul Kadir, the then Deputy Minister of Human Resources previewing my second book: "Performance Management & Measurement the Asian Context". With my colleagues Karen Ong and Jeremy Spoor.

At the launch of our software HRDPower, the web version in 2008 by His Excellency Datuk Seri Dr S. Subramaniam, the then Minister of Human Resources, Malaysia.

Colleague Sahiran Shuib with Gabriel Nyeholt presenting the implementation of HRDPower to Tan Sri Yukio Morishita, Chairman of Matsushita Corporation, Japan

In one of the several assignments in Brunei

Training at the Bahrain Institute of Banking & Finance

The Accredited Training Professional programme, Kuala Lumpur, Malaysia

Karen Ong, our Master Trainer and Director, continuing the FUN training journey

Subra, our Principal Consultant and Chief Executive, continuing the Competency Journey.

1999, the first opportunity to train in India, with the ICICI Bank.

The training that accelerated my journey in 1986, with British Petroleum.

Learning to sign as an author, good feeling to be asked to sign your book. How true: there is a book within everyone waiting to be written.

Training senior executives from Hewlett Packard Philippines.

Participants from Macau, one of the 35 countries I have now worked in.

Shifting gears, the first of the many keynotes at the Indonesian Association of Training & Development

Launching the first Malaysian Training video in 1994, produced by colleague Lisa Vincent

Jim Kirkpatrick, son of Prof Don Kirkpatrick, our former colleague and then Vice President Training, SMR USA who initiated our US operations

The enthusiastic Asia HRD Congress team

1st Malaysian Certificate in Training & Development (UK) 1984

Diploma in Training &Development, 1990.

CHAPTER 5

Lessons Learned from Life Experiences

. . .

This book is not about how successful I've been – that's not the point. I'm not a billionaire, a Nobel laureate, or an Olympic gold medallist. I'm a very ordinary person, the perfect outsider in most cultures.

I've had the opportunity to be friends with people who have gone on to become parliamentarians, ministers and even presidents. Some of them have made significant contributions while some have languished. I also have friends who make important contributions to the society and are deemed successful, even though they are not in high positions. Success is not about medals or positions. In simple terms, it is about achieving the goals you set for yourself. There are millions of ordinary people who go on to achieve success the way they define it and they do it because they have learned some important lessons from life experiences. They are happy as they choose to be happy.

If we do not process our experiences and learn from them, we will make very little progress. Peter Drucker, the famous management guru says, "Mistakes occur but do not let them recur." Highlighting the importance of life experiences as a teacher, author Tom Bodett differentiates thus between school and life: in school you are taught a lesson and then you take a test, whereas in life, you are given a test that teaches you a lesson. In the same vein, Bob Pike the well-known trainer's trainer, points out that while children learn in order to pass a test, adults learn to make a living.

I have learned several lessons from my experiences in this global journey as a professional trainer, HR consultant and entrepreneur. I set myself a direction, some goals and went about trying to achieve them. I've had a variety of experiences and I've tried my best to learn from them. I've repeated many mistakes and taken a long time to learn sometimes, but ultimately I did. The point I want to make here is that going on a global journey doesn't have to be difficult. It is easy, provided we are willing to learn. I'd like to discuss some common sense principles and personal and business lessons that I've found extremely useful along the way.

Power of Self - Discipline

The first lesson I learned on my global journey was the need for self-discipline. It is said, "Self-discipline is an act of cultivation. It requires you to connect today's actions to tomorrow's results." Self-discipline comes from knowing that a season for reaping follows the one for sowing. Winston Churchill is said to have remarked, "We often do things that we like to do rather than what we ought to do." The things that we do not want to do are the very things that we need to do the most. "How easy it would be if exercising was as easy as eating," said an author. Why don't we do certain things that we know we could or should do? We all have good reasons, but they don't often make sufficient excuses. If we have to spend time on certain things, whether it is spiritual pursuits, physical exercise, reading and learning or family, then we have to do it. I learned the hard way to be disciplined in doing what I need to do, though it wasn't easy to make it a part of myself. The Jesuit priests, my teachers, taught me how to wake up every morning at 5.00 am and exercise every day for an hour. They helped me develop good habits that are sustained by self-discipline and goals.

Due to the tremendous focus on growth all the time, the goals I set for myself have been different at different periods of my life. Initially it was growing as an individual, then finding our place in the training world as a small organisation and finally, managing the growth of a public listed company.

*"We often do things that
we like to do
rather than
what we ought to do."*

Winston Churchill

To see myself through all these different phases, I found self-discipline to be an important asset.

When I was starting out as an entrepreneur, I had this experience with Professor Rajalingam, an outstanding Professor of Finance. We went to Sabah to work with a Government Linked Corporation. He was the consultant and I was the coordinator. The 60-year-old Professor was particular about where he stayed, but also cost-conscious. We stayed at a five-star hotel due to its close proximity to the customer's offices. It was expensive and we were paying for it ourselves, but I told him it wouldn't be appropriate for him to stay anywhere else. He said if I didn't mind, we could share the same room so that I could save costs. When we had customers, we would entertain them for lunch at the hotel, though it wasn't by any means cheap. When we were by ourselves, for dinner or coffee, he suggested going out to a local coffee shop. He said, "When we have lunch with a customer, it's a business cost. When we have a cup of coffee, just you and me, it's a personal cost. You need to be able to differentiate between a business cost and a personal cost. A cup of tea in the decent nearby coffee shop is probably ten times cheaper than at a five-star hotel. You should have the personal discipline to differentiate between needs and wants and between personal costs and business costs." That was an invaluable lesson for me particularly during the start-up phase. Professor Rajalingam taught me much more than the need for financial prudence. He underlined the need for self-discipline. Through the years, I could have afforded a bigger car or a bigger house on debt but I had learned the need for planning and prioritising.

Benny Ong, a Singaporean friend leads a financial advisory firm called Life Planning Associates. I learned from him the absolute necessity to be debt-free. The learning has been so ingrained in me that I tend to miss the fine line between financial discipline and risk aversion. There are times when our analysts look at our figures and ask why our debts are low compared to our assets and I quip that it comes out of emotional baggage. I am still wary of debt, because I had to struggle with debt after the loss of our family business in Myanmar and my father's untimely death. I learned the need for financial prudence and self-discipline from these two fine gentlemen. Everyone agrees that self-discipline stands one in good stead, but practising it is the hard part. However, it is the practice that keeps you focused on what needs to be done rather than what you would like to do. Harry S. Truman said that while reading the lives of great men and women, he noted that the first victory they won was over themselves. Self-discipline came first for all of them.

Power of Passion

The second lesson in my global journey is that to be successful one does not need an Ivy League education or be born with a silver spoon. Many people have gone on a global journey *powered only by their passion* to create value.

Consider Konosuke Matsushita, the founder of Panasonic or Narayana Murthy, the co-founder of Infosys. Matsushita was born into a well-to-do family, but his father lost his fortune, resulting in a life of poverty for the family. Matsushita was not able to continue his education beyond the age of nine. Despite having no money or education, he leveraged his experience in the electrical industry to set up his own company. He struggled, but eventually came through purely because of his passion to create value and contribute to society. Take the case of Narayana Murthy of Infosys. He co-founded Infosys in 1981 with an investment of 10,000 Rupees (less than 550 Ringgit Malaysia) from his wife, Sudha. In a few years, Infosys went on to become one of the largest wealth creators in the country. He changed the face of Indian business for the world through innovative and ethical practices. When the company hit a crisis in the late 90's he offered to buy his co-founders out but they decided to stick together and face the storm. He still serves as an inspiration to so many would-be entrepreneurs in India. Matsushita is a global brand and Narayana Murthy paved the way for India to become a global software powerhouse. It was their passion to create value that made them household names.

We often hear the name of Roger Bannister in

motivational circuits. Roger Bannister, a young medical student, was passionate about running. At the 1952 Helsinki Olympics, he set a British record for 1500 meters but he failed to win the medal he was hoping for. To make up for the disappointment, he was determined to run one mile in less than four minutes, a feat deemed impossible in those days. Bannister trained with passion. The historic moment came on May 6, 1954 at the Iffley Road Track, Oxford. He ran the mile in 3 minutes and 59.4 seconds and the result was greeted with loud cheers from onlookers. His record lasted only for about a month and half and proved that the four-minute barrier had no real significance except in the minds of people. With the psychological barrier broken, within months, others went on to break Bannister's record. But Bannister will remain as the one who showed the world that it was possible to run a mile in less than four minutes.

The power of passionate belief in a cause helps you to break limitations that people set for themselves. I love what Steve Jobs said: "Your work is going to fill a large part of your life, and the only way to be truly satisfied is to do what you believe is great work. And the only way to do great work is to love what you do. If you haven't found it yet, keep looking. Don't settle. As with all matters of the heart, you'll know when you find it. And, like any great relationship, it just gets better and better as the years roll on. So keep looking until you find it. Don't settle."

Staying True to One's Purposes and Values

The third lesson that I learned was the need to *stay true to one's purposes and values.* One can succeed no matter what the environment is. When I first came back to Malaysia after my initial studies in India, everyone told me that the days for Malaysian Indians to work as HR professionals in Malaysia were over. I was told I would not be able to find a good job in the HR profession. On that count, the only place to get a HR job would have been in a plantation as that was the only place with a majority of Malaysian Indian employees then. Many people told me what cannot be done; very few helped me to look at what could be done. I wanted to be in a profession that helped people learn and perform at the workplace. Among the few who helped me redefine the way the game is played was a mentor named Samuel Abishegam, a founding member and a past president of the Malaysian Institute of Human Resources Management. He helped me check out the various options available to me.

Bringing in overseas labour was one option because that was good money. The others included running employee services such as transportation or staff canteens, working in a Malaysian Indian owned company with a majority of Malaysian Indian employees, or joining the Civil Service. None of these options appealed to me.

Sam Abshigam helped me remain determined and

"Your work is going to fill a large part of your life, and the only way to be truly satisfied is to do what you believe is great work. And the only way to do great work is to love what you do. If you haven't found it yet, keep looking. Don't settle.

As with all matters
of the heart,
you'll know when you find it.
And, like any great
relationship,
it just gets better
and better as the years roll on.
So keep looking
until you find it.
Don't settle."

Steve Jobs

stay true to my core purpose which was to make a valuable contribution to the HR community. My late father always used to say, "Son, if you want to have a swim in the sea, you can never swim without the waves." Life will continually throw up challenges. The thing to do is to go out there staying true to your purpose and redefine the way the game is played. After a couple of jobs, I became an entrepreneur in the business of helping people learn and perform at the workplace.

A lot of people talk about Steve Jobs as though computers were the purpose of his life. But he never saw it that way. He wanted Apple to make life more productive for people through their easy-to-use solutions. He had a '**digital hub**' strategy. Similarly I don't see SMR as a human resources business. Rather, I see SMR in the business of helping people be competitive, employable and capable of making a contribution. We want to develop a Learning Hub.

Choosing to be Happy

A young man on the Obama campaign team introduced me to the 2004 book *The Paradox of Choice: Why More Is Less* by American psychologist Barry Schwartz. This book is based on the premise that despite having more choices, people feel less happy. Schwartz's studies have shown that American consumers today have far greater choices than they had five decades ago and yet there is a high level of unhappiness. Schwartz argues for eliminating consumer choices to make people feel happier.

The campaign specialist and I started talking about choices during an election campaign. The debate between American democracy and Asian ones that are more guided took us to a discussion about the different promises made by the candidates. Voters seemed to have more choices but there was the troubling thought that they were still unhappy. It is worth asking if the well-being of an individual truly depends on having greater autonomy and freedom of choice.

How one goes about making a choice also has an impact on happiness. Schwartz refers to two types of people when it comes to making a choice – maximizers and satisficers. Maximizers are perfectionists who need to be assured that their choices are the best that could be made. This is certain to be a daunting task given the extensive research that would go into checking out all the options. Satisficers, on the other hand, set some criteria and as soon as they find a product or service that fits the criteria, they make a choice without worrying too much if there could have been a better option available. Making a choice is certainly less exhausting for satisficers.

One of the ingredients for happiness then is a clear idea about the standards and criteria by which we define what we want. As I had described earlier in the book, friends like Dr. Nat and Ed Jackson asked me time and again, "What is it that you want?" They realised that my happiness depended on my awareness of what I wanted and the standards and criteria I was willing to settle for.

Choosing to be happy in an abundant world full of people who never seem contented was my fourth lesson. Four theories dominate the studies on happiness: First there is the hedonistic view that happiness is a matter of raw subjective feeling. According to this view, a happy life maximises pleasure and minimises pain. Second, there is the desire theory that views happiness as a matter of getting what you want. In this perspective, it is the gratification of a desire that leads to happiness. Third, the objective list theory places happiness within a list of things that matter. This view holds that happiness consists of worthwhile achievements. Finally, there is the authentic happiness theory that views happiness as an outcome of a meaningful life. Consider the struggles of Nelson Mandela or Aung San Suu Kyi. Happiness arises from having an engaged and meaningful life.

The first step in choosing to be happy is to have the intent, a conscious choice to be happy. The philosopher Bertrand Russell remarked: "Happiness is not, except in very rare cases, something that drops into the mouth, like a ripe fruit. Happiness must be, for most men and women, an achievement rather than a gift of the gods, and in this achievement, effort, both inward and outward, must play a great part."

Gretchen Rubin, the author of *Happiness Project* talks about her year-long experience in test driving the wisdom of the ages, current scientific studies and lessons from popular culture

*"Happiness is not,
except in very rare cases,
something that drops
into the mouth,
like a ripe fruit.
Happiness must be,
for most men and women,
an achievement rather
than a gift of the gods,
and in this achievement,
effort, both inward
and outward,
must play a great part."*

Bertrand Russell

on happiness. When we are happy, we manage our emotions and relationships better, a key requirement for achieving better results. Her readings and experiences highlighted the fact that the only person whose behavior she could control is herself. Rubin says that in choosing to be happy you focus on doing meaningful things that make you happy. She says, "Making little changes in your life can have a dramatic impact on the happiness you feel on an everyday basis." Rubin says happiness is voluntary and within the reach of everyone.

Tony Hsieh, the CEO of Zappos, in his book *Delivering Happiness* says it is important to create fun and a little weirdness for a company's success. Happy employees work better and are superior performers given that all other variables are of course in place. I find it strange that some people are never content and never happy. They are always in search of some elusive thing. When enough is never enough, corruption is often the result.

There were many instances when I was on the brink of giving up on my entrepreneurial journey. The only thing that kept me going on was my personal commitment to be happy and to do what mattered to me most. The reason I kept on going was because it was something I thought was meaningful to me while adding value to society. As my good lawyer friend says, "It is important to pursue meaningful things and at the same time have a good night's sleep."

Power of Thinking Big

There were many friends who continually tried to get me to think big. A person who needs to be mentioned here is Mr. Ahmad Pardas, the former Chairman and CEO of UEM Malaysia, a large conglomerate. He has probably never realised the impact he made on me. I had only met him a few times in the company of another mentor and fellow director Haji Ishak Hashim. When we were about to take our company public for an Initial Public Offering to be listed on the Mesdaq Market of the Malaysian Stock Exchange (BMSB), he told me about the book *The Magic of Thinking Big*.

I've learned so much from the book. That one book has made a huge difference to me personally, in providing my fifth lesson: The Power of Thinking Big. My former colleague Robert Lim used to always remind me that if I wanted to grow a global corporation, then I had to let go of operations and manage the strategic part. I never understood the significance of this advice until another good friend of mine challenged me. As I have described earlier, the concept of Big Hairy Audacious Goals (BHAGs) proposed by Jim Collins and Jerry Porras in their 1994 book, *Built to Last: Successful Habits of Visionary Companies* made a huge impact on me. They defined a BHAG as a strategic business statement which is created to focus an organisation on a single medium to long term organisation-wide goal which is audacious, likely to be externally questionable, but not internally regarded as impossible. They said such a move encourages organisations and individuals to come up with visionary goals. Such goals are more strategic and emotionally compelling than tactical and short term. As examples, we have Aung Sang Suu Kyi who wants to liberate Myanmar or Prof. Mohammad Yunus of the Grameen Bank in Bangladesh who created the world's microcredit revolution. The legendary Tom Peters, co-author of *In Search of Excellence* applauds Jim Collins for the concept of BHAGs.

The whole idea of thinking big took me a long time to learn. Being successful on a global journey requires BHAGs. Before listening to my friends talking about BHAGs, I had no clue about the concept of thinking big. After discovering BHAGs, I realised that when I strived to grow the company, I was averse to taking risks and had a tunnel vision restricting us to the HR space. I realised I had to get out of the tunnel vision.

We started looking for opportunities to grow, to scale the business and develop multiple streams of revenue. One such opportunity we explored was bidding for tenders. While this was a competitive space, competing with world class companies raised the bar for us. Most countries have huge tenders. We took the risk and participated in these huge global tenders despite the massive investment of effort, time and finances. We were exhilarated when we won about five or six tenders that gave us a tremendous financial boost. We grew into a multimillion dollar corporation. We moved beyond corporate management development to vocational, language and information technology training. These growth areas fit within our core business area and the aspiration of helping people learn and perform at the workplace.

We learned to get into long term contracts to enable us to focus on long term value propositions. To achieve this goal, we had to let go of jobs at the lower end of the value chain. This meant we had to abandon things that inhibited or obstructed our growth. I'd like to relate the story of a company called SuccessFactors started by Lars Dalgaard. He pioneered cloud computing which was initially championed by SalesForce.com. In the days of large HR enterprise systems from SAP and Oracle/Peoplesoft that consumed huge capital expenditures, he focused on developing a new model in the industry. He focused on creating software as a service and came up with cloud computing models in the HR space. The concept of making customers pay a monthly subscription and converting huge capital expenditures into operating expenditures was welcomed by cost-conscious organisations. His goal was to make every organisation afford a people management tool. Pundits decried his approach and many wrote him off. The business was set up in 2001, a time when technology companies were facing the worst crisis. Lars Dalgaard plodded on despite massive losses for he was sure he was making a valuable contribution. The company was losing 3-4 million US dollars every year. Within the space of a few years, his organisation covered hundreds of thousands of employees. In 2011, he sold his company to SAP for 3.4 billion US dollars. The story of SuccessFactors reflects a long term compelling value proposition that seemed not feasible at the outset. It took 10 years for Lars Dalgaard to see his goal realised. My fifth lesson was learning how Big Hairy Audacious Goals hold the seeds for business success.

Power of Information

Marshall Goldsmith said, "What got you here won't get you there." It didn't take me long to realise that what got me to be a reasonably successful trainer or consultant was not going to be good enough for me to become a reasonably successful entrepreneur. Do I want to be an entrepreneur? Do I find it a meaningful pursuit? Would I be happy in being one? Do I have the passion to create value as an entrepreneur instead of being a self-employed professional? What do I mean by reasonably successful? There were hundreds of questions crowding my mind. Honestly, I had no answers to most of them but I was determined to take the message of helping people learn and perform to a wider audience. While Marshall Goldsmith talks of many ideas in his practical and thought-provoking book, the one thing I realised soon was for the need to change with changing times.

With the help of close friends, I recognised the need to make certain shifts with changing times and changing roles. Unless we are willing to learn and constantly keep our minds open to new information, we are not going to be able to make those shifts. I don't really know how many people in business really read the budget or how many of them are aware of what the government's policies are, but I am aware that a lot of people criticise the government for what it doesn't do. But if you actually read the budget, there are so many things in there that can prompt an entrepreneurial mind into action. For instance, I learned to find out how much is allocated for education and human resources development. Sometimes, the government all of a sudden opens up a certain field, say, in education, manufacturing or technology. When we access the information, we are able to evaluate if this is something that we want to do. This information is available in the public domain, yet it is amazing how few know about it. Very few access the information that is available in the public domain, a fact that works to the advantage of those who take the trouble to find out. The one who has the information has the competitive advantage. Either you need to be able to do something first, which is the first-mover advantage or you must have the operational capability to imitate someone very well. As an entrepreneur, you have to overcome the notion of "information assymetry". This simply means very few people have access to the key information.

Once we ran a series of nationwide conferences for Malaysian Indian entrepreneurs as part of the government's initiative to transform the Indian community and make it easy for them to do business. While we were going around and sharing the principles of business and entrepreneurship, a movie clip shown by one of the speakers caught my attention. It was an interesting clip that clearly highlighted the power of information. The film clip shows a young educated man whose fortunes take a turn for the worse. He takes refuge in a temple. An old homeless man sleeps in the temple every day. The young man goes up to him and asks him if he knows of any jobs he could take up. The old man obviously has no advice to offer on that but he says, he doesn't have a job to offer but he could ensure that the young man has three good meals every day. So the old man wakes the young man up early next morning and directs him to a temple for breakfast. The young man goes there to get the food and gets back only to be sent around noon to another temple for lunch. The same happens at dinner and the next day. The young man, being a young graduate, gets so demotivated and screams at the old man, "It is because of people like you that the country is in so much trouble. Don't you have a sense of shame and embarrassment? You go and beg at all these temples, eat every meal and just sleep. Isn't it just a pitiable state? Now I don't think I have to work with you. Because I can just go to these very same temples myself and get the food and do something worthwhile for the rest of the time." And the old man responds, "That's precisely the point. You won't be able to do it because between the two of us, only I know which temple serves food on which days." The question is: Is that hiding information? No, it is not, it is available to all who seek it. But one man has gathered the information from different places, tracks it regularly and follows a plan of action and the other is dependent on him.

For example, all the information on opportunities for entrepreneurs is available in the public domain, but only some of us access it and a large majority do not. Some see the opportunity but do not do anything about it. The ones who find success are the ones who collect and use the information wisely. This was my sixth lesson.

Power of Networks

I think it is impossible for anybody, whether you are an entrepreneur, a trainer or a consultant, to know everything in life. You need networks where people communicate with you. You need people to give you information about the changes happening out there in the world. I think there are moments when you have an idea; it is of no use till you act on it. Stephen Covey stressed on the importance of being proactive. It is a common sense principle, but he explained it so well in his book, *The Seven Habits of Highly Effective People*.

Once I was telling Datuk Kasi, a prominent Malaysian architect and builder, about the trouble I was having running a business in India. In the course of our conversation, he asked me, "Palan, do you know that in Malaysia we have a board for listing new technology companies?" That was an idea I had heard before but not acted upon. Now, his words pushed me to pursue with company secretaries, auditors, and financiers and from these sources, I collected as much information as I needed from other friends on my network. I realised that to be publically listed, I would need a team of experts because I knew I couldn't do it. None of the people I had with me could do it. So we went and hired people with the expertise to see us through the process and we went public. Once we went public, we got to know that there were new things to learn and comply with.

I was convinced of the power of networking quite early on and now with social media it has become much more powerful. My seventh lesson was the realisation that we need networks to help us connect and communicate for creating value for the individual and the organisation.

The Ability to Say "No"

I must admit I couldn't bring myself to say 'No' for a long time and even now am occasionally unable to say a decisive 'No'. Honestly, this has been my biggest weakness. My eighth lesson is that it is critical to say a clear 'No' when it is required. Diederick Stoel, one of my friends from the Netherlands, calls me a 'sub-assertive' person. I get very stressed when I agree to something not because I want to or that is the correct thing to do but to protect the feelings of the person who made the request. It has been an expensive lesson for me.

There are lots of people out there who just can't say 'No' and suffer because of that. One thing I admire my Western friends for is that in general, they are much better at making their stand clear than Asians. There are many cultural studies that outline the reasons for it. Geert Hofstede cites the uncertainty avoidance index, while others have pointed to high context and low context cultures.

While we may all understand the various cultural dimensions, it is challenging when you suffer the consequences of not saying 'No'. It is so much easier when someone says 'No' because then you know exactly where they stand. You won't go around thinking they had agreed to something when in fact they hadn't. You won't have to wait for months and figure out that they weren't interested when they don't return your calls. When I look back on my own life I've found that most of my losses have happened because I couldn't bring myself to say a simple 'No'.

Am I more comfortable in saying 'No' now? Personally I have enormous difficulty denying a request, but in my current role as a Chairman or CEO of a company I sometimes have to. Luckily, I am in a position of luxury today because I've people who can say 'No' for me. Even if I didn't have that luxury, I've learned that if you are considered a sharing and generous personality, people will accept it when you turn down a request. That's why it is important to create emotional bank accounts as Stephen Covey has mentioned. I think you can never grow when you are trying to satisfy everybody. But there are certain relationships that are very important in life, which brings me to the topic of managing diversity and then work-life balance.

Engaging a Diverse Workforce

One of the outcomes of having a global presence is that I've had to hire from different parts of the world. Their terms of engagement are different. Sometimes the cultural nuances of interaction are very different from what you are used to. At SMR, we have people from 26 countries. Sometimes they don't necessarily agree with what I have to say. As an entrepreneur who has grown from running a business on my own, I kind of get perturbed when someone disagrees strongly. I then take a step backward and tell myself that the reaction is based on their perception of what was said. That is a perception and perceptions are unfortunately real and therefore I'll have to rethink and reconnect with these people with the networks and information available to me. My ninth lesson is that engaging a diverse workforce is critical because growth demands a global outlook.

Work – Life Balance

I was intrigued to read an opinion that there is no work-life balance; there are only work-life choices and that leads to my tenth lesson. One of the biggest challenges I've faced in my global journey has been my inability to maintain a work-life balance. There was always so much to achieve because of the passion I had for growing the company. But there was a downside to it. My former colleague and Master Trainer Jeremy Spoor used to tell me often not to forget that my boys are going to grow up very fast. True enough, one day I turned around and my boys were taller than I. I had missed out on their school holidays and concerts and they've always been closer to their mother than to me. Unfortunately there is no magic formula to fix this situation. I thought I would make an effort to catch up when my daughter was born. Over the years I've found that it hasn't worked either. She is also closer to my wife. My daughter would always ask me, "Dad, are you going to send me to school today?" or "Will you come to pick me up from school?" And, my answer had been always pretty standard, "Darling, I have a business meeting."

One significant life-changing experience for me was watching a 15-minute video by Steve Jobs on YouTube. I watched Steve Jobs delivering his Stanford University commencement address **'How to live before you die?'** He talks about three things: connecting the dots, love and loss and death as a change agent. His talk revolves around the ideas of linking disparate things, doing what you love and recognising that death is a change agent. The question that provoked me was "What would you do if today was the last day of your life?" After watching that video, the next morning, I got up early and took my daughter to school. While I realise that I cannot be involved in all the activities of my children, I understand the need to be present in the defining moments of their lives.

Work-life balance is really about work-life choices and that includes living in the moment. My friend Uday Khedkar reminds me all the time to not forget that the ***moment is now***. The Steve Jobs talk reminds us to look into the mirror every morning and respond to the questions, "Am I doing what I like to do?" and "What would I do if today is the last day of my life?" In general, I've learned that it is important to keep revisiting your personal goals on a regular basis. Eckhart Tolle pointed out that the Power of Now is so important. If anybody said they have a perfect prescription in life for work-life balance, it would largely be a lie. We just have to work on the work-life choices to find a balance.

In conclusion, we all have lessons gained from our life experiences. The key to a successful journey is to apply the lessons in our life for us to grow into better human beings. I have shared some common sense principles from my experiences gained in this global journey. Undoubtedly, you would have some of yours to add. The goal is to learn and grow.

CHAPTER 6

Global Journey — Challenges and Insights

. . .

My forefathers migrated from India via Burma (Myanmar) to Malaysia more than a hundred years ago when there were not many travel facilities. They took the risks like many of the thousands of Indians who migrated to different parts of South East Asia did. Their global journey was far more challenging than mine. They left for new shores to find markets and bring back to the home country a quality of life that was not otherwise possible. They were interested in trade and not on localisation. Therefore my forefathers always retained their culture and comfort zones. Today of course, migration is so common and people find it easier and sometimes necessary to blend in with their new environments.

I grew up in Malaysia, a country I truly consider I

belong in and one that has given me many opportunities. My global journey has taken me beyond the shores of Malaysia and its culture. It has also required of me to grow beyond my 'Indianness' without losing the heart and soul of the culture. I am a product of many cultures, a fact that has caused me a certain level of identity crisis. My family was convinced that I was westernised, despite my best efforts to not give that impression. My counsellor friends trace my dislike to say 'No' and be assertive to my cultural roots, though some others say it is a refusal to learn. Culture is dynamic, requiring us to adapt to different parts of the world while retaining our cultural roots.

Some time back I went to a Tamil concert. My first reaction was regret in having missed out on some of the philosophies and richness of literature all these years due to my business priorities. On reflection, I realised that the priorities in our lives change as we grow. We have the option of revisiting things that we may have missed out during an earlier phase.

Such conflicts are not uncommon in the globalised world impacted by technology and change. On hindsight, to me this global journey is about my learning experiences, being happy when my goals are achieved, being myself in a world that thrives on change and still remaining relevant in a changing world. It is about how I was able to move beyond the shores of Malaysia in search of new markets – an entrepreneurial journey.

Some of you may choose not to move beyond Malaysia. That is fine. You may not even move out of your little town. That is fine too, as long as you keep in mind the impact of global developments on your own little world. It is important to realise that globalisation is not about globetrotting, but about understanding the impact of happenings in one part of the world on another and in turn, the impact they may have on you as an individual and on your career or business.

Let's take the example of the impact of the revolution in telecommunications that we are witnessing today. Smartphones and related applications allow us to communicate for free across the world. In some parts of the world, places that never had access to landlines have now gone straight on to using mobile phones. So if you go to India or China, you will notice that everybody has a mobile phone, even in places where there are no fixed telephone lines. The explosion in the outreach of global telecommunications has changed the dynamics of life even in remote villages. This has opened up the world, resulting in expressions such 'the global village'.

Or let's say I want to open a restaurant in my town. I'll have to take globalisation into consideration because young people in my town may expect a certain type of food, presented in a certain way as a result of their exposure to the world. Thus, whether you step out of your town and country or not, our journeys are no longer insular. They are impacted by global trends. You may experience the impact of globalisation even if you never stepped out of your house. Your children may go to study abroad and come back with an outlook born of a different culture.

The comfort zone that my forefathers enjoyed by retaining their cultural roots in a different country is not always relevant in today's world. There were several challenges that I faced on my journey and I wish to share my insights on how I dealt with them.

Looking Beyond Familiar Shores

In my case, my global journey started with looking beyond Malaysia with a fierce drive to take the message of 'making learning FUN' to the world. My first stops were nearby countries such as Singapore and Brunei, which allowed me to remain in my comfort zone because not only is it adjacent to Malaysia, it is also very similar culturally, despite the global competition so prevalent there. It was a high value market from a business perspective yet one that was highly competitive. Then I went to Indonesia, Thailand and the Philippines, thus covering most of the ASEAN (Association of South East Asian Nations). All these countries shared some similarities with Malaysia. Going from one country to another, I was gradually able to move away from my comfort zone.

Then, thinking my ethnicity would help, I ventured

into India only to realise that India was as diverse as the world can be. My inability to speak Hindi was a drawback but the cultural similarities and the widespread use of English in the country helped me. I learned that when dealing with different countries and cultures, the key to achieving your business goals lies in recognizing the differences and identifying similarities that can be leveraged.

Then I went into the Middle East, Hong Kong, China, Australia and the USA. My journey covering over thirty countries was launched to find new markets and grow the business. Little did I realise the competitive challenges or the preparation, planning and understanding required. Let me share some of my experiences.

In September 2000, when we launched our software in Dubai, it marked our first stop in the Middle East. Dubai was fast becoming the financial capital of the Middle East. As a part of the United Arab Emirates, a member of the Gulf Cooperation Council (GCC), Dubai was thriving. Getting a foot in there was a prerequisite for success. At the same time, it required courage and staying power because it was a big investment for us and we didn't get our first job till after ten months. Our going to the Middle East was due to the efforts of the former Prime Minister of Malaysia, Tun Dr. Mahathir Mohamad who developed great bilateral relations between the two countries. He opened up the markets for Malaysian products and organisations and went on a drive to create Malaysia as a brand. The Malaysian Ministry for Tourism, at that time led by Minister Tan Sri Abdul Kadir Sheikh Fadzir, spearheaded the campaign *Malaysia, Truly Asia*. The country was projected as a progressive Islamic country, economically stable, where people of different races and religions are able to live peacefully.

Moving in line with the trends – the opening up of the Middle East markets to Asian economies, the post 9/11 scenario, the consistent push for Malaysian exports and the global economy – enabled us to get a foothold in Dubai first, and later in Abu Dhabi and Sharjah. Then we went into Bahrain, Qatar, Saudi Arabia, Oman and Kuwait. Now we have a presence in all the six countries in the Gulf Cooperation Council (GCC). There were many challenges in that we had to understand each country and its cultural diversity. Each country had its own share of expatriates – Egyptians, Syrians, Jordanians, Palestinians, Algerians, Pakistanis, Indians and Westerners from different countries – with their own ways of working. There was more diversity there than anywhere else we had been before. For example, at that time there were more than 105 nationalities working with Emirates Airlines, considered one of world's best airlines.

We were aware that we no longer enjoyed the advantages of competing on home soil and were no longer insulated from global competition. As we moved from country to country in the GCC, we realised that the best form of advertisement is always word of mouth.

An Asian Company with a Global Outlook

Playing in a global market requires you to deliver what you say you will deliver consistently. This is in line with the maxim, 'You do not get a second chance if you do not get it right the first time.' You will have to compete with the best in order to succeed. If we evaluate how we fared in the markets we served or how globally competitive we are, it will be fair to say that we have competed with the big names in HR consulting and succeeded in competitive tenders. Given our size and our depth of capabilities, we've been able to hold our own against some of the world's best. Not just in Malaysia or in Brunei or Indonesia, but in various Asian markets.

We haven't penetrated significantly yet into the USA or Europe because the cost of doing business in these countries is horrendously high for us. Still, we consider ourselves a global player. Let us say, if an organisation has a large operation in Hong Kong and they are looking at all the global players and you are among the bidders, then you are not just an Asian company, you are a global player and that's what SMR has done.

The only question asked is, "Are you able to add value to our organisation and its bottom line?" Our goal has always been to position ourselves as an organisation that offers a value proposition of helping people learn and perform at the workplace. No one cares if you are Asian or Western. What competitive organisations need are solutions that add value to their efforts. While a global journey forces us to look beyond our shores, we need to have a value proposition that is attractive to the new markets.

I believe that Asia has got much to offer the world. Unfortunately over the last couple of centuries, we have sort of lost our thought leadership. The West has invested significant time and effort in research and development (R & D) and they have made a good job of selling their ideas. The thought leadership and communication efforts of the West far outpace Asian efforts. If you go into a bookshop or a library, you will find a disproportionate number of books written by Western authors. There is nothing wrong in that because knowledge deserves respect regardless of where it originated. It is just that while we learn from the West, we must not forget that there is much in the Eastern cultures that we can still learn from and take to the West. The Indian spiritual gurus helped Beatles and Steve Jobs, the programmers from Asia helped propel information technology companies to newer horizons and the Japanese and Chinese showed the way with superior manufacturing processes. We live true to the maxim – an Asian company with a global outlook and a compelling value proposition.

Branding

Branding is very much influenced by one's cultural background. For example, in the USA, they say you must have a high profile, or if you come from a strongly Buddhist background, you might want to remain very modest with a low profile. To me, branding is not just about maintaining a low or high profile. It is about standing out in the crowd, being recognised for something you are good at. You don't have to shout about it, but have your customers recognise you for it. This is the compelling value proposition that I talked about earlier.

My goal was really for our customers to associate a FUN training style with me. I wanted to be recognised for pioneering FUN learning. Famous trainers are recognised for their specific contributions: Ed Scannel is recognised for Games Trainers Play, Stephen Covey for Seven Habits, Kirkpatrick for Training Evaluation and Thiagi for Training Games and Small Groups. The size of the market in which you are recognised is immaterial, as long as it covers the field that you want to operate in. You might find that somebody is recognised in a particular field in your country but not necessarily in another country. The power of a brand rests in the quality and influence of thought leadership that it provides in a field. We've been able to position FUN training tools, *The Magic of Making Training FUN!!*, HRDPower, the Competency PAGE framework, Trainers Meet Trainers and Asia HRD Congress as our recognisable brands in the field of people development. We did it at a great investment of time, effort and money, but eventually we were able to differentiate ourselves from other companies, at least in the markets we serve.

One of the challenges in building a corporate brand has been to separate the individual from the brand. I've been asked if FUN is the brand or Palan. When we started off, for years together, I was the brand. It was challenging because I found that I had to be in the training room 250 days a year to generate any revenue. At that time, it was fine because I was in Kiyosaki's **S** (self-employed) quadrant and enjoying it. I was directly touching lives and that in turn raised my self-esteem. I felt good about it, but soon I was getting burnt out because I was doing too much. I was involved in so many training programmes that there was no time for even processing the learning from these training programmes into usable frameworks for the future.

This was unsustainable and I deliberately stepped back from the centre stage. We formed a community of accredited trainers, created a plug-and-play training model, and now I have colleagues who can independently deliver the FUN training as well or better than I. I have been able to move on to focus on other things.

One of the things that I have learned is that we have to

let go in order to grow. Steve Jobs is reputed for making Apple succeed with very few products. They say the first thing he did after taking over was to trash many products that did not add value to the organisation.

I used to work with a great airline for over six years. It was a tremendous asset to have them on our client profile. The problem was that as I was the brand ambassador for SMR, the customer would not let anyone else deliver the programmes. Can you imagine the late Steven Covey running the programme globally all by himself? It was not only unsustainable, but also not a good business model. We were not able to focus our efforts on building the brand, something that requires much work outside the training room too. Inevitably, as we grew, we had to let go of this client.

Today we have been able to create a consistent methodology so that even though individual styles differ, the value creation does not vary from trainer to trainer.

Inflection Points
In attempting a global journey, it is important to understand the inflection points. We can recognise an inflection point when we are able to observe critical game changers.

When I was growing up, I observed that people liked to carry a transistor with them when they went on picnics.

Years later, the Walkman replaced the transistor. It became the fashion of the day. People would put it in their pockets and they had cassettes that held about 20 songs. Later the cassettes were replaced by CDs. Then, the MP3 players came along. Napster appeared on the scene and everybody started downloading music. At Apple, Steve Jobs wondered how they could make these downloads legal. So Apple entered into a partnership with recording companies, which allowed their music to be downloaded legally and they made it pretty easy with iTunes. You could now download a song for about 0.99 cents or an entire album for 9.99 US dollars. Customers now had a choice to buy only the tracks that they wanted. They found the technology easy to use and cost-effective. The recording companies found that they could prevent illegal music downloads.

There was an MP3 player around already, so it wasn't that the technology was new. Lots of people had access to the technology. It is just that Steve Jobs observed the market, identified a need and capitalised on that need. And the rest is history. It changed the fortunes of a company like Apple and it was a win-win for everyone. Apple won, the consumer won, the recording companies won, the artistes won. The beauty was that nobody lost. The philosophies were very straightforward – make it easy for the customer, give the customer the choice, and make it a win-win for everyone. You may ask questions about the Paradox of Choice that we discussed in the last chapter. Yet, Apple offered customers a choice but also structured the choice in a way. I think of it as a good demonstration of the power of observation.

I read a story in the Harvard Business Review. It was about Steve Jobs' biographer Isaacson talking about Jobs reaction to market surveys. When an executive proposed a market survey for identifying customer needs, Jobs was reported to have said: "Customers do not know what they want." It was for them to find out what the unsatisfied and undiscovered needs of the customer were.

When I went into Brunei the first time, I observed that the country was a greenfield of opportunities. This country with plentiful resources was keen on getting its people ready to face the future. Brunei had gained independence from the British in the early 80's and was enthusiastic and eager to embark upon a learning journey. The patriotic citizens wanted to prove to the world that they were ready for independence. It was the right time to go in with productivity training programmes. Very few competitors were there at that time, but today when the country has a very well-developed infrastructure, there is a long list of providers. There is a saying that luck is when opportunity and hard work meet. Sensing the right moment to enter a market is critical for business success and so you will find a number of expressions such as 'first mover advantage' and 'joining the bandwagon' in the business dictionary. First movers are those who anticipate the need, understand the inflection points and make the first move.

Power of Scanning the Environment

Entrepreneurs, visionaries and business leaders identify inflection points by scanning the environment. The formidable rise of Air Asia and Tony Fernandez underlines the importance of the power of scanning the environment for opportunities and for deciding the right time to act. Tony Fernandez spotted an idea – Ireland based Ryanair was doing very well in low-cost flying. He established Air Asia in December 2001 when his company Tune Air Sdn Bhd bought over the debt-ridden airline business from DRB-Hicom.

Using the power of networking, he sought an appointment with the Prime Minister, convinced him and took over the airline with its several million debts for 1 Ringgit Malaysia. Lots of other people knew about the opportunity, but did not have the guts to take the risk. He took the risk, got the business model right and 10 years later, he has over 100 planes and employs around 10,000 people. He didn't create low-cost travel. He didn't conceptualise it. He scanned the business environment and realised that the time was ripe for a low cost option in flying. Today he refers to Air Asia not as a Malaysian airline, but as a regional airline. They are in Thailand, Indonesia, Philippines and India. People said Air Asia can't fly into Singapore. So it flew into Johor Bahru, Malaysia and operated a bus service to Singapore. The Singapore Government stopped the bus service by withdrawing the bus license. It was an attempt to protect the local airline but with the open skies policy, Air Asia could fly direct to Singapore. Of course, Air Asia Japan failed, but it did not deter Air Asia in any way.

If we take a look at the low cost airport terminal in Kuala Lumpur, we see the many thousands of people whose lives have undergone a positive change because of the entrepreneurial streak of Air Asia led by Tony Fernandez and team due to the power of scanning the enviroment. The Malaysian venture gradually expanded to other countries. That is a global journey. It is not somebody going on a holiday to 80 countries. I think that is the essence of the blue ocean strategy.

Yet, when you ask Tony Fernandez the reason for Air Asia's success, he ascribes it to the workforce. Yes, he does that, he scans the environment to spot diamonds, which are then polished for value. He says he sometimes spots talent in unconventional places. In a conference session, he related the story of spotting one of his stars, then a baggage handler, at the Sibu airport when he was supporting his team by handling bags. He does it once in a while so that his staff can talk to him. The baggage handler underwent pilot training to become a Captain at Air Asia.

Choosing the Right Partner

When you go global, it is important to know who you should partner with while entering unfamiliar territories. There was a time when we thought the company was doing well and all was smooth sailing. So we decided to move to the next level and get into a developed market to tap into one of the world's largest markets for technology. We were mainly trying to establish our software HRDPower in the international market. I realise now that to enter a new market, you need a partner with a tremendous knowledge of the local market. They have to be an insider to make up for the fact that you are an outsider.

We decided to work with a friend only to find out it was a disastrous partnership. There are several points for us to consider when we choose a business partner. Some people may be suitable for you as friends, but they don't always make the best business partners. Unfortunately, we haven't always been good at making that distinction.

Our partners were very hospitable people and they shared our dream of creating value. However, we failed to evaluate their skill set from a business perspective. The fact that they did not have a game plan and did not want to commit to one was a red flag that we failed to notice. If your partner doesn't know the market and refuses to get to know it or worse still, does not want to put pencil to paper to draft a plan, it is time to get out of the business relationship. In life you will find that when you are not ready internally, any external factor can affect you pretty badly. The year 2008 saw one of the worst economic recessions globally. The company suffered one of its biggest losses ever to a point it looked like we might even go out of business. We made a quick rearrangement of what we and our partner wanted to achieve and quit that market.

I've lost out rather badly twice mainly because I chose the wrong partner for the market. They were good people but not suited for the world of business. The legendary Lee Iacocca, former Chairman of Chrysler Corporation, USA, said that a wrong choice of partners not only stops you from pursuing your journey, but results in your getting deviated from your plan. It takes you years to get back on track.

That was when I realised the global journey does not mean setting up operations in every part of the world. It means having a presence which is not necessarily a market share, but a mind share, so that everybody recognises you for one or two things. Jack Welch's philosophy is very true. You've got to be No.1 or No.2 in the markets you serve. If not, he said: "Fix it, sell it, or close it." So I might just serve in a small market which might be Brunei, but I should be No.1 or No.2 in that market. Your partner should be able to support you to reach that goal – with market knowledge, relationships, networks and financial support. One definite way for risk mitigation on a global journey is to choose the right partner.

The Importance of Agreements

Most of the time when we analysed a business problem, we could trace it back to the fact that the parties involved

"Fix it, sell it, or close it."

Jack Welch

either did not have a clear understanding of the job or that the understanding was not put in writing.

When I went to the US, which is a very low-context culture, I dealt with a transaction lawyer who got to the point straightaway and asked, "Palan, can we sign this agreement?" I said, "Sure we'll do it tomorrow." And the lawyer said, "Palan, you and I are friends and because we are friends, let us agree and put that agreement in writing and it will help us preserve our friendship." Low-context cultures value structure and systems.

Arab cultures are more high-context than Western cultures, which is to say relationships account for much more in these countries. We found that the people do not like conflict or direct confrontations and hold values similar to other Asian cultures. Communication and personal relationships are so very important. While contracts in the Middle East are usually large, it may not be the easiest of places to do business for those who do not understand the local culture. We found that people hesitate to sign contracts and when they do, it takes them quite long to do so, possibly because one's word is considered good enough in the Arab culture.

Once again, I learned something important on the cultural front. A global journey requires an understanding of different cultures, but that does not mean you should let it affect your business transactions. I have found that in business and personal life, it is important to have a clear agreement. In the Middle East, contracts are all about trust and it is not considered important to codify trust on paper. In a low-context culture, trust is equally important, but the stand is, "Since we all trust each other, why don't we put it on paper?"

Whether high-context or low-context, the lesson is to adapt to the culture as far as possible and ensure we have an agreement in place. You may differentiate what you say and how you say it, but I cannot emphasise enough the importance of agreements wherever you work. If you come across markets which do not honour the agreements signed, then all of us know the answer. It is best to avoid that market. You also have to look out for the availability of a fair legal mechanism to address grievances, such as arbitrations in a neutral third country.

The SMR team is an outstanding one; they are an integral part of this journey.

Remembering what my grandparents taught me: Corporate Social Responsibility.

A truly great learning environment with great faculty. Proud to be part of it.

With fellow directors: Dr Nat, Hj Ishak Hashim, Kamu, Venky and Leow Nan Chye.

Wrap Up

The passion to go global is fine. However, passion alone is not enough. The legendary author and adult educator Thiagi says passion alone gets you nowhere. We need tools and resources. We should be clear about what we want and why we want to go global. Is it to create a brand, propel a value-based message or create value for shareholders? Some markets are more lucrative than others but we should ask if that is the only reason to go there. Are we willing to observe and learn from the world's best to be best in class ourselves? Till we compete with the world's best, we won't be anywhere close to being world class.

To me global journeys are not just about the pursuit of individual achievement. The question of societal contributions carries equal weight. Quality of life and monetary success are by-products of the journey. In a world that is increasingly becoming wrapped up in individual success, I worry whether we are losing one of the basic tenets of Asian cultures – that of contribution to society. The emphasis on winning at all costs, be it in business and education, or on reality television shows, makes me nervous about the future.

It was in this context that I was overjoyed to hear about the success of Asian mountain climbers. Raha Moharrak is just 25 years old, the youngest Arab and the first Saudi woman ever to climb Mount Everest. I was elated to hear Raha comment to the press: "I really don't care about being the first, so long as it inspires someone else to be second." She inspires us to keep challenging our own standards. Close on the heels of this exhilarating news, came another about six Malaysian climbers reaching the summit of Mount Everest. That one of them was a 23-year-old woman makes the occasion more memorable and clearly reminds us that the glass ceiling can be broken and prejudices are all in the mind. The Malaysian climbers reached the summit two days before the 16th anniversary of the first time the Malaysian flag was planted on the summit in 1997. At the press conferences hosted for the climbers, each one of the climbers talked about the months of gruelling training, both physical and mental. Malaysian journalist Mazlinda Mahmood said, "The pain is temporary but the pride lasts forever."

The success of the climbers calls for celebrations. It

tells the world what achievers do differently from others. The world thrives and grows on hope and success stories. Scott Friedman, Past President of the National Speakers Association went around the world researching best practices of the world's leading organisations in order to make them known to the world. When Roger Bannister ran the mile in less than four minutes, his success gave hope to many.

As I wrap up my story, five terms that were extraordinarily important for me stand out in my mind. They may apply to anyone who is an entrepreneur, professional or employee. Trust, Emotional Intelligence, Leadership, Feedforward and lastly, Humility are the five significantly important terms.

Trust binds you to your customers. My Jesuit teachers always told me that it takes a long time to build trust, but only a few seconds to break it. Trust is the foundation for human relationships. The story of a little girl and her father crossing the bridge is a poignant one. The father asked his daughter: "Sweetheart, please hold my hand so that you don't fall into the river." The little girl said, "No, Dad. You hold my hand." The surprised father asked, "What's the difference?" "There's a big difference." replied the little girl. "If I hold your hand and something happens to me, chances are that I may let go of your hand. But if you hold my hand, I know for sure that no matter what happens, you will never let go of my hand." In all relationships, the author says, the essence of trust is not in its bind, but in its bond. It is vital that we hold the hand of the person we work with rather than expect them to hold ours. Trust is a mutual process, but we have to take the lead and build it with our stakeholders. In this global journey, trust was my key companion.

To build trust you need emotional intelligence. It is a life skill. I have been stunned in my global journey to find an abundance of it at times and a near total absence of it at other times. Dan Goleman popularised emotional intelligence (EI). He suggested that the emotional brain responds much faster to an event than the thinking brain. Dan strongly notes about the importance of EI: "If your emotional abilities aren't in hand, if you don't have self-awareness, if you are not able to manage your distressing emotions, if you can't have empathy and have effective relationships, then no matter how smart you are, you are not going to get very far." We must appreciate the essence of what David Caruso said: "Emotional intelligence is not the opposite of intelligence, it is not the triumph of heart over head – it is the unique intersection of both." It is a myth that emotional intelligence is just being nice to everyone. On one of my journeys to the UK, I was intrigued to read a story penned by Oliver Burkeman in the Guardian Weekend. The story takes place in London during the tube strike in 2007. "A journalist named Gareth Edwards is standing with other commuters in a long, snaking line for a bus, when a smartly dressed businessman blatantly cuts into the queue line behind him. (Behind him: this detail matters.) The interloper proves immune to polite remonstration, whereupon Edwards is seized by a magnificent idea. He turns to the elderly woman standing behind the queue-jumper and asks her if she'd like to go ahead of him. She accepts, so he asks the person behind her, and the next person and the next – until 60 or 70 people have moved ahead, Edwards and the furious queue-jumper shuffling further backwards all the time. The bus finally pulls up and Edwards hears a shout from the front of the line. It's the elderly woman addressing him: "Young man! Do you want to go in front of me?" How little it takes for us to be emotionally intelligent! I have been careful to cultivate EI in my global journey and I must admit that I am still learning.

Leadership is such an overused word today. Yet, it somehow cannot be undervalued; it is this extraordinary thing that leads to goal achievement. I have realized the importance of thought leadership, people leadership, ethical leadership, business leadership and customer leadership in my entrepreneurial journey. Ralph Nader, the American consumer advocate, remarked that the role of a leader is to produce more leaders not more followers. You lead the way for others to become trailblazers themselves.

British climber, George Mallory, was often asked why he wanted to climb Mount Everest. Tired of the same question again and again, Mallory finally answered: "Why do you want to climb Mount Everest–my answer is simple, because it is there. Everest is the highest mountain in the world, and no man has reached its summit. Its existence is a challenge. The answer is instinctive, a part, I suppose, of man's desire to conquer the universe."

Feedback is a word often used in executive coaching and behavioural change programmes. Giving and receiving feedback in behavioural terms is seen as part of the learning and growing up process and is considered a life skill. I have wanted to know on a real time basis if I was doing something right or wrong. However, feedback would only talk about something that has already happened. In that sense, it is limited and static. It is in this context that Marshall Goldsmith suggested the simple but powerful tool–'feedforward.' It is an experiential exercise where each participant is asked to play two roles. One involves providing feedforward, where they give companions suggestions for the future and help as much as possible. In another role, they accept feedforward, by listening to suggestions for the future and learning as much as possible. It is always about suggestions for the future and not about the past. Feedforward is important as it is based on the premise that we can change the future but not the past. The focus is on solutions and the task–nothing is personal.

Last but not the least, humility is a very important value for a person to learn and grow. In my global journey, the awareness that I had so much to learn from the world out there always had a humbling effect on me. You can learn a great deal from the world. However, it only happens when your feet are firmly planted on the earth. Rabindranath Tagore, the great Indian poet said, "We come nearest to the great when we are great in humility."

Being humble, accepting feedforward, providing leadership, being emotionally intelligent and building bridges of trust were certainly building blocks in my global journey.

As I step back and reflect upon my years in business, I can only think about the joys of life. Yes, there were many challenges along the way, fears about failure, at some points no money to pay the bills and occasionally, nagging self-doubt. Yet, I've immensely enjoyed this journey that I started with a capital of few dollars. Significant milestones have been crossed, but the journey will continue as long as the passion and purpose last. Over the last three decades, I have learned much from some great people whose insights and knowledge have been splendid torches that lighted my way on this journey. Today we do not have to wait for three decades to learn essential life skills for our journey, with technology enabling the easy sharing of knowledge and experiences.

I have enjoyed the sharing immensely. Whatever little I could do to make this world a better place for at least a few people, I have done. So this is what I'd like to leave you with.

As our parents told us to look both ways before we cross the street, I urge you to look at the purpose of your life. Robin Sharma stated simply, "The purpose of life is a life of purpose." Focus your energies on what you would really love to achieve because when you do so, you will enjoy the journey and cherish the joy of living. As the legendary Tamil poet Thiruvalluvar said: "Learn well whatever is worthy of learning, then act according to that learning."

Epilogue

. . .

The story of this global nomad was not without twists and turns. My lasting memories of this journey are made up of many uplifting surprises, crushing disappointments and enduring joys. It was a learningful journey.

On February 9, 1975, I sobbed uncontrollably when my father died – not only because he was gone from this world, but because I had not yet told him how much he meant to me and how much I loved him. I had missed many moments to tell him how precious he was to us. I learned the importance of the Power of Now, then.

In June, 1976, I again wept unashamedly, standing on the steps of a medical college when I chose to give up on my dream of becoming a doctor, again not because I could not afford it due to my dad's demise nor because I could not achieve the status symbol of being a doctor, but because I could not fulfill my childhood dream of serving the poor and needy in search of healthcare. I learned the value of being passionate about what you care, then.

June 26, 2013, was another defining moment in my life when SMR secured shareholder approval to acquire Cyberjaya University College of Medical Sciences (CUCMS). CUCMS is a specialised medical university college with an outstanding faculty. An eight-year-old institution with current strength of about 1500 students and 200 faculty members, CUCMS is an institution with great character. I learned I could still contribute towards caring for those in need of healthcare.

July 1, 2013, was an emotional day for me as I visited CUCMS and addressed the faculty and students. I realised and learned that we now had the unique opportunity to develop world-class doctors and touch the lives of millions of people in more positive ways than I could ever have imagined. Living the SMR motto of helping people learn and perform would be even more satisfying now.

Again, in the midst of overwhelming joy, I was fully aware of the toil and sweat of countless number of people who pushed me along on my journey. Never before did I realise the full impact of the words 'God's work on earth must truly be our own.' It does not really matter if you did not start out the way you wanted to, what matters most is if we can live the spirit and essence of what we wanted to be.

Now I have the unique opportunity to live the CUCMS motto: Nurturing the passion to care.

And, for me, the learning journey continues.

Oops, not my successor,
she is set on her learning journey
just as I am set on mine...
The Learning Journey continues...

Selected References & Recommended Reading

Branson, R. (2008). *Business stripped bare: adventures of a global entrepreneur.* London: Virgin Books ;.

Burlingham, B. (2005). *Small giants: companies that choose to be great instead of big.* New York: Portfolio.

Chopra, D. (1994). *The seven spiritual laws of success: a practical guide to the fulfillment of your dreams.* San Rafael, Calif.: Amber-Allen Pub. :.

Collins, J. C. (2001). *Good to great: why some companies make the leap–and others don't.* New York, NY: HarperBusiness.

Covey, S. R. (1989). *The seven habits of highly effective people: restoring the character ethic.* Melbourne: Business Library.

Dayao, D. L. (2000). *Asian business wisdom: lessons from the region's best and brightest business leaders.* Singapore: Wiley.

Drucker, P. F. (1985). *Innovation and entrepreneurship: practice and principles.* New York: Harper & Row.

Ferriss, T. (20112007). *The 4-hour work week: escape 9-5, live anywhere and join the new rich* (Expanded and updated ed.). Chatham: Vermilion.

Friedman, T. L. (2005). *The world is flat: a brief history of the twenty-first century.* New York: Farrar, Straus and Giroux.

Gladwell, M., & Gladwell, M. (2000). *The tipping point: how little things can make a big difference.* Boston: Little, Brown.

Godin, S. (2003). *Purple cow: transform your business by being remarkable.* New York: Portfolio.

Godin, S. (2008). *Tribes: we need you to lead us.* New York: Portfolio.

Goleman, D. (1995). *Emotional intelligence.* New York: Bantam Books.

Goss, M. (2012). *What is your one sentence?: how to be heard in the age of short attention spans.* New York: Prentice Hall Press.

HBR guide to finance basics for managers. (2012). Boston, Mass.: Harvard Business Review Press.

HBR's 10 must reads: the essentials. (2011). Boston, Mass.: Harvard Business Review Press.

Harvard Business Review on succeeding as an entrepreneur. (2011). Boston, Mass.: Harvard Business Review Press.

Hsieh, T. (2010). *Delivering happiness: a path to profits, passion, and purpose.* New York: Business Plus.

Hupalo, P. I. (1999). *Thinking like an entrepreneur.* W. St. Paul, MN: HCM Pub..

Isaacson, W. (2011). *Steve Jobs.* New York: Simon & Schuster.

Joel, M. (2009). *Six pixels of separation.* New York: Business Plus ;.

Joel, M. (2013). *Ctrl alt delete: reboot your business. reboot your life. your future depends on it.* New York: Business Plus.

Kim, W. C., & Mauborgne, R. (2005). *Blue ocean strategy: how to create uncontested market space and make the competition irrelevant.* Boston, Mass.: Harvard Business School Press.

Kiyosaki, R. T., & Lechter, S. L. (2000). *Rich dad, poor dad.* New York: Warner Books (US).

Kotter, J. P. (1997). *Matsushita Leadership: lessons from the 20th century's most remarkable entrepreneur.* New York: Free Press.

Livingston, J. (2007). *Founders at work: stories of startups' early days.* Berkeley, CA: Apress ;.

Marketing and Entrepreneurship - DonLoper.com. (n.d.). *Marketing and Entrepreneurship - DonLoper.com.* Retrieved October 16, 2013, from http://www.donloper.com/

Marr, B. (2012). *Key performance indicators: the 75 measures every manager needs to know* ([1st ed.). Harlow, England: Pearson Financial Times Pub..

Meyers, H. M., & Gerstman, R. (2007). *Creativity: unconventional wisdom from 20 accomplished minds.* Basingstoke, Hampshire: Palgrave Macmillan.

Moss, D. A. (2007). *A concise guide to macroeconomics: what managers, executives, and students need to know.* Boston, Mass.: Harvard Business School Press.

Murthy, N. R. (2009). *A better India, a better world.* New Delhi, India: Penguin Books India :.

Natarajan, B. (1980). *Economic and political philosophies of Thiruvalluvar.* Madras: ITES Publications.

Obama, B. (2008). *The audacity of hope.* Edinburgh: Canongate.

On the Record With ... Nandan M. Nilekani. (2004). New York: Conference Board, Inc..

Palan, R. (1997). *The Magic of Making Training FUN!!.* South Carolina: Advantage Media Group.

Palan, R. (2008). *Creating Your Own Rainbow.* South Carolina: Advantage Media Group.

Ramasastry, C. S., & Menor, L. (2004). *Dabbawallahs of Mumbai.* London, Ont.: Ivey Pub.?].

Ramos, F. V. (1997). *Leadership for the 21st century: our labors today will shape our country's future.* Manila: Friends of Steady Eddie.

Rubin, G. C. (2010). *The happiness project.* New York: HarperCollins ;.

Ryan, E., & Conley, L. (n.d.). 10 Intriguing Business Books for Entrepreneurs to Read on Vacation | Entrepreneur.com. *Business News & Strategy For Entrepreneurs | Entrepreneur.com.* Retrieved October 16, 2013, from http://www.entrepreneur. com/blog/222423

Sheppard, M. (1995). *Tunku, his life and times: the authorized biography of Tunku Abdul Rahman Putra al-Haj.* Petaling Jaya, Selangor Darul Ehsan, Malaysia: Pelanduk Publications.

Sonnier, L. (2009). *Think like a marketer what it really takes to stand out from the crowd, the clutter, and the competition.* Franklin Lakes, NJ: Career Press.

Tao: *the three treasures : talks on fragments from Tao te ching by Lao Tzu.* (1976). Poona: Rajneesh Foundation.

The Toyota Foundation: 30 years of history 1974-2004. (2007). Tokyo: Toyota Foundation.

Warrillow, J. (2011). *Built to sell: creating a business that can thrive without you.* New York: Portfolio Hardcover.

Wasserman, N. (2012). *The founder's dilemmas: anticipating and avoiding the pitfalls that can sink a startup.* Princeton, N.J.: Princeton University Press.

Wawge, R. S. (2008). *National happiness: thinking beyond GDP.* Hyderabad, India: Icfai University Press.

Weidlein, M. S., & Roth, S. F. (1992). *Empowering vision: for dreamers, visionaries & other entreprenuers* (2nd ed.). Boulder, CO: Aimari Press.

Welch, J., & Lowe, J. (1998). *Jack Welch speaks: wisdom from the world's greatest business leader.* New York: J. Wiley & Sons.

Wenger, E. (1998). *Communities of practice: learning, meaning, and identity.* Cambridge, U.K.: Cambridge University Press.

APA formatting by BibMe.org.

About the Author

Palan, a Malaysian, is an entrepreneur by choice. He considers himself a nomadic wanderer with a lifelong mission to create value for people, organizations, communities and societies. He is passionate about helping people learn and perform.

An alumnus of the Harvard Business School, Palan studied in USA, UK, Australia, India and Malaysia. He has authored over 15 management and human resource books. He is presently the Chairman of SMRT Holdings Berhad, a company listed on the ACE Market of the Bursa Malaysia Securities Bhd. The company has three operating divisions: HR Professional Services, HR Software and Education.

He has worked internationally for over three decades in 30+ countries though his focus is very much Asian. More details at www.palan.org

Printed in the USA
CPSIA information can be obtained
at www.ICGtesting.com
JSHW012026140824
68134JS00033B/2891

9 781599 324876